Contents

About the authors

Mark Fairweather is a practising solicitor, and is one of the founding partners of the legal firm Fairweather Stephenson & Co. He is co-author with Rosy Border of the Stationery Office's *Simply Legal* series of DIY law kits as well as several titles in the *You Need This Book First* series. He has two children and lives in Suffolk.

Rosy Border has worked in publishing, lecturing, journalism and the law. She is a prolific author and adapter who stopped counting after 150 titles. Rosy and her husband, John Rabson, live in Suffolk and have a married son in Tennessee.

Welcome

Welcome to the *You Need This Book First* series. Let's face it – the law is a maze. This book is your map through the part of the maze that deals with making your will. It contains everything lawyers would tell you about making your will, if only they had time (and you had the money to pay them). And if you follow our advice you should end up with a will that

- does what you want it to do
- is legally sound
- you as a non-lawyer can understand.

Acknowledgements

A glance at the *Useful Contacts* section will show how many individuals and organisations we consulted while compiling this book. Thank you, everyone. We would also like to thank John Rabson, Chartered Engineer, for his IT support, research and refreshments.

We put you in control

This book

- provides the general information that professional advisers would give you on the subject, if only they had the time, and if only you had the money to pay them
- tells you the buzzwords that are important in this section of the law, and what they mean
- provides plain English wills to meet most needs
- answers some of the most frequently asked questions on the subject
- is supported by a website that is regularly updated.

This book empowers you. That is a good thing; but it means responsibility as well as power. Think of yourself as a driver using a road map. The map tells you the route, but it is up to you to drive carefully. Watch out for the road signs along the route.

Hazard signs

We tell you when you are in danger of getting out of your depth and need to take professional advice. Watch out for the hazard sign.

Legal lore

Sometimes we pause to explain something: the origin of a word, perhaps, or why a particular piece of legislation was passed. You do not need to know these things to make use of this book, but we hope you find them interesting.

–Power points

Sometimes we pause to empower you to do something: watch out for the symbol.

Clear English rules OK

We draft WYSIWYG wills – *w*hat *y*ou *s*ee *i*s *w*hat *y*ou *g*et.

Legal documents have traditionally been written in archaic language, because this wording has stood the test of time – often several centuries – and has been hallowed by the courts. What is more, the use of technical language can sometimes enable specialists to express esoteric concepts in a kind of professional shorthand that is useful to them but meaningless to others.

The use of archaic language is, however, unnecessary and may be dangerous. The worst problem is that for non-specialists it is a foreign language, unknown at worst and incompletely understood at best, with all the potential for misunderstanding which that entails.

Why write your will in a 'foreign language' in preference to plain English? What is important is that your will is expressed in clear, unambiguous language that accurately reflects your intentions.

A will is sometimes said to 'speak from death'. In other words, it deals with your circumstances on the day you die, *not* the day you make your will. Unless you write your will on your death-bed, the problem this raises is that you have to express your wishes without knowing what the situation will be like when you die. For example, you do not know what you will own, or whom you will leave behind, at the time of your death. The art of good will drafting is to achieve precision in the context of this uncertainty. Of course, this is also a good reason to review your will regularly, (we tell you how, on page 90).

On the (fairly rare) occasions when we *do* need to use technical language, we offer clear explanations (see *Buzzwords*).

Get it right – obey the rules!

All the same, to be valid, a will must comply with certain formalities about signing and witnessing (see *Signing your will* on page 85). As any lawyer will tell you, a will that is defective could generate more legal fees than no will at all.

Wills on the web

Check out our website. Purchase of this book entitles you to access our exclusive readers' website.

www.youneedthisfirst.co.uk

Six bad reasons for not making your will

There are six excellent reasons for making your will. First, however, here are some of the reasons people give for *not* making their will:

- **'I can't make up my mind who's to get what'**

  Well, you could always make a will that gives someone else the power to make the decisions after your death. This is called a *discretionary trust* (see *Buzzwords*). If you don't make a will at all, your estate will be divided by law according to rules that will take no account of your personal wishes (see *intestate* in *Buzzwords*).

- **'Nobody makes a will at my age'**

  Oh yes, they do. Anyone who is over 18 and of sound mind can make a will.

Legal lore

Sixteen-year-olds in the armed forces can make valid wills, on the basis, perhaps, that if they're old enough to die for their country, they're old enough to decide who should inherit their assets.

- **'They can slug it out among themselves when I'm gone'**

Is that really what you want? Apart from the anger and bitterness, think of the solicitors' bills.

- **'Pull the other one – I haven't anything worth leaving'**

You'd be surprised how much you may be worth, especially when you're dead! In any case, wills aren't just about possessions; for example, they can be used to appoint guardians for children.

- **''Er Indoors will get it all anyway'**

It ain't necessarily so, especially if you and 'Er Indoors ain't legally married! A co-habitee that has lived with you for two years can make a claim, but this is a recipe for expensive, stressful disputes.

- **'I'll do it when I'm not quite so busy'**

  And when will that be? Far too many people put off making a will until it is too late. People who die intestate – that is, without making a valid will (see *Buzzwords*) – can leave a time-consuming, heart-breaking, expensive muddle for their families.

Six good reasons for making a will

Consider these:

- By making a will you can make sure your estate goes to the right people in the right proportions, thereby avoiding family quarrels and expense.
- If you and your partner are not married, it is vital to make a will; otherwise your partner, however long you have been together, may get a raw deal. And if you are in a same-sex relationship, the law as of today provides no protection at all.
- If you and your spouse are separated but not divorced (by decree absolute), unless you make a will to the contrary, they may well inherit your estate.
- You can choose your executors – the people who will carry out the instructions in your will – for yourself.
- You can give great pleasure to people dear to you by leaving them keepsakes or small gifts, and you may even be able to right some past wrongs.
- You may be able to reduce the amount of Inheritance Tax payable.

What if you don't make a will? The diagram below shows what will happen.

What happens if you don't make a will

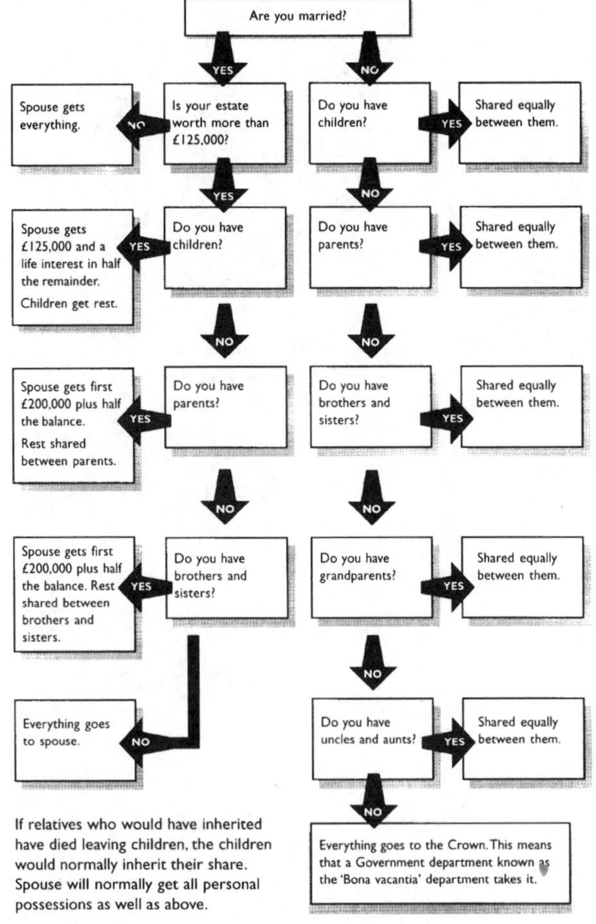

If relatives who would have inherited have died leaving children, the children would normally inherit their share. Spouse will normally get all personal possessions as well as above.

NB This table is an outline of the rules as they apply in England and Wales. Adapted from: Which?, June 1991, published by Consumers' Association

You should note that your spouse's fixed net sum is payable free of Inheritance Tax (see page 36) and costs, and attracts interest from the date of your death until the money is handed over.

Buzzwords

asset – anything you own which is of value.

beneficiary – someone who inherits under a will.

bequest – something left in a will (the verb is *bequeath*; but *give* is usually just as good).

Court of Protection – the court that makes orders for the management of the financial affairs of people who do not have the mental capacity to do this for themselves. The *Public Guardianship Office* (see below) is the executive agency that implements these orders.

deceased – lawspeak for dead.

discretionary trust – a form of trust that lets the trustees (see below) decide who gets what.

Enduring Power of Attorney – the legal power that you give to someone so that they can handle your financial affairs if you become mentally incapable of doing so.

estate – this might mean your rolling acres or the family Volvo, but in this context it means everything you leave behind after you die.

executor – a person appointed in your will to sort out your affairs after you die. (If you do not make a will, the person who sorts out your affairs is called an administrator.)

Legal lore

The feminine form of *executor* is *executrix* (plural *executrices*); but, thankfully, executors are unisex nowadays (see also *testator/testatrix* below).

guardian – the person you nominate to have *parental responsibility* (see below) for your children under the age of 18 if you die AND their other parent is also dead OR does not have parental responsibility. Your children's guardian will have the same responsibilities and powers as a parent.

intestate – without making a will; **intestacy** – the state of being intestate.

legacy – something left in a will; the recipient of a legacy is sometimes called a **legatee**.

life interest – a situation in which an asset will be owned by the trustees, but the beneficiary will have the use of that asset and/or the income from it for their lifetime. Life interests are complicated and definitely not a DIY option – seek professional advice rather than trying to do something fancy on your own.

lifetime gift – a gift made during your lifetime.

living will – an advance request not to be kept alive artificially in circumstances where you do not have mental capacity to refuse treatment AND your quality of life is very poor AND there is no hope of recovery.

mirror wills – wills which come in matching pairs: for example, between husband and wife. A mirror will is not necessarily a mutual will.

mutual wills – wills which represent a binding contract between two or more people, by which each says in effect, 'I'll do a deal with you. I agree to make a will like *this* in reliance on your promise to make a will like *that*.' The point of a mutual will is that it cannot be changed without the agreement of the other testator – either before or after the death of the first to die. In practice most mutual wills are mirror wills, but it is not necessary for them to be so. Mutual wills cause problems. For further details, see page 140.

parental responsibility – the responsibility which by law a parent has for their child and the child's property. This concept was introduced into the law by the Children Act 1989.

pecuniary – to do with money, eg **pecuniary legacy** – a gift of money.

Legal lore

Pecuniary comes from the Latin *pecunia* – money – which in turn comes from *pecus*, which meant a flock or a herd in the days when your livestock were your wealth. Now you can bore people at parties.

probate – the official recognition (technically a court order) after death that the will is valid and confirmation of the executors' authority to administer the estate; a **grant of probate** is the document that confirms a will is valid.

Public Guardianship Office – the executive agency that is responsible for the financial affairs of people whom are unable to manage them for themselves (see also *Court of Protection*, above).

real estate – a useful Americanism for land and bricks and mortar.

residuary – to do with the residue (see below).

residue – what is left over after paying off any debts, expenses and legacies of money and specific items.

revoke – cancel (a previous will); every will should contain a **revocation** clause to establish that it is the last will.

spouse – the unisex word for 'husband or wife'. No, we don't like it either, but 'partner' is ambiguous and 'husband or wife' is cumbersome.

survive – outlive someone; live on after someone has died; **survivor** – a person who has outlived someone; **survivorship** – the state of being a survivor.

testamentary – to do with wills – e.g. *testamentary capacity* – the mental capacity to make a will; *testamentary expenses* – the expenses incurred by your executors to carry out your instructions in your will.

testator – a (formerly male, now unisex) will-maker.

trust – a legal entity which imposes a duty on someone – the **trustee** – to own and manage assets for the benefit of someone else – the *beneficiary*; see above – usually on a long term basis. An executor is a form of trustee with specific, short–term responsibilities relating to the administration of the dead person's estate.

And here are some buzzwords which we don't use, but which you may have found elsewhere.

administrator – the person who winds up your estate if you do not appoint an executor.

chattels – moveable property, as opposed to land or buildings.

codicil – an extra clause added to a will – a sort of PS and not advisable for amateur will-makers.

issue – descendants.

personal representative – the generic term for an administrator or executor.

per stirpes – providing for a gift to pass down in equal shares to the next generation, so that if a beneficiary with children dies before the testator, the deceased beneficiary's children inherit in their stead.

Legal lore

Per stirpes comes from the Latin *stirps – stirpis,* a rootstock and, by extension, descendants.

predecease – die before.

Frequently asked questions

I'd like my husband/wife to be my executor, but I'm worried that he/she might not be able to cope on his/her own. What can I do?

Make sure your spouse has access to good advice. If your spouse is sole executor, he/she does of course have full control. If having control will not be important to your spouse, appoint a second executor in your will (see *Executors* on page 48) to share the load. Do get their agreement first, however.

If I don't make a will, does everything go to the Crown?

Only if you have no living relatives when you die. The diagram on page 9 shows how the intestacy (see *Buzzwords*) rules work. Making a will is particularly important for people living together outside marriage because the intestacy rules take no account of unmarried partners.

Can I appoint someone who is bankrupt as my executor?

Yes. But might they be tempted to run off with the money?

—Suppose I appoint trustees to look after my children's inheritance and guardians to take parental responsibility for them – how do the two groups interact?

Try to avoid this scenario – it's a lot easier if the guardian has access to the money. If this is inappropriate (for example, the guardian is a loving parent substitute but hopeless with money), the terms of the trust should enable the guardian to have access to funds for the children's maintenance and education.

—Can an executor be a beneficiary?

Yes.

—How would divorce affect my will?

A decree absolute cancels all benefit from the will in favour of your ex-spouse. There is a trap here, however. If you die between the irretrievable breakdown of the marriage and the decree absolute, your spouse will benefit either under your existing will or under the intestacy rules. It is vital, therefore, to make a new will as soon as you are sure there is no hope for your marriage (see *Marriage and divorce* on page 62).

—Does the law treat adopted and illegitimate children the same as legitimate children?

Yes. Furthermore, the intestacy rules and Inheritance (Provision for Family and Dependants) Act 1975 (from here shortened to Inheritance (etc) Act) also protect an unborn child.

Legal lore

Where an embryo is fertilised with the sperm of a man who has died, that man is not in law the father of that child. For legal purposes, the child is fatherless, unless subsequently legitimised or adopted.

What happens if my executor dies before me or is sick, living abroad or otherwise unable to act for me?

Provide for a substitute executor in your will.

What if one of my beneficiaries dies before me?

A gift to someone who dies before you will normally lapse. If the gift is a legacy (see *Buzzwords*) the money or asset in the gift will fall into the residue of your estate. If the gift is part of the residue, there may be an intestacy (see *Buzzwords*) of that part of the residue – depending on the wording of your will. It may be appropriate to make a substitutional gift, which is a gift to somebody else in the event of the beneficiary dying before you (we show you how on page 133). There is one exception – if you make a gift to your child or grandchild, who then dies before you, the gift will pass automatically to that person's own children unless you specify otherwise.

—What happens if a beneficiary cannot be found?

The executors must first make reasonable efforts to find the missing person, although how far to go will depend on the circumstances and the value of the gift. This may usually involve newspaper advertisements or instructing an enquiry agent. If the beneficiary cannot be found, the safest option for the executors is to obtain a court order authorising distribution on the assumption that the missing beneficiary died before the testator. For small gifts, the executors can dispense with the court order and pass the gift to someone else – provided they promise to return the gift if the missing person turns up.

Obviously, a testator should seek to avoid this situation altogether. One way to do so is for the will to specify the steps that the executors must take to find the beneficiary, such as no more than three letters to the last known address.

—I want to leave my house to someone. Are there any problems?

There certainly are! Here are just a few.

- If there is a mortgage, who pays it off?
- Is the gift to be free of Inheritance Tax?
- What happens if you sell the house before you die, or do not even own a house when you die?
- What happens if you own two houses when you die?
- What happens if at the time of your death you have exchanged contracts to sell the house and/or to buy another house? Which one are you giving away?

- What happens to the contents of the house?

And if you are thinking of giving your children a share of the house which you own jointly with someone else,

- can you actually give it in your will, or will your share pass automatically to the surviving joint owner?
- will the children be joint tenants or tenants in common between themselves and with the other co-owner? (see *Legal lore* on page 42.)
- will the children have the right to live there?
- will the children be able to force the house to be sold?
- and, if the house is sold will the children be required to use the money to re-house the surviving co-owner?
- who pays for the repairs and insurance?
- who pays the council tax?
- Will the children be happy to pick up the Capital Gains Tax bill on any profit from sale (if, as often happens, it's not their main residence).

If you are still hell-bent on this course of action, please take professional advice.

— What arrangements can I make for my pets to be cared for after my death?

Under the Animals Act 1971 a pet is classed as a domestic animal and is a personal possession. You can therefore leave your pets to someone in your will. Because some pets are costly to keep, you could also leave some money to defray future expenses. Either leave money to the intended recipient of the pet, or set up a trust fund that will have an income to cover the costs during the pet's lifetime. It seems that a trust for a pet must be limited to a maximum of 21 years (which is tough on tortoises). In practice, do not take someone by surprise with a gift of a pet!

— How do I alter or add to my will?

What you *can't* do is cross things out or add things in, or add PSs to an existing will after signing. You can in theory add a codicil (see *Buzzwords*) and get it properly signed and witnessed (see page 86); but in these days of personal computers it is much simpler and safer to make a new will. Your *last* – this is, *latest* will is the one that applies.

— My partner and I are both male. Can I leave everything to him?

Of course; and we give an example of a will which does this. In fact, you are wise to make a will in his favour, because without one he would get nothing. Note that a same-sex partner is not able to make a claim under the Inheritance (etc) Act (see page 59) unless he or she is financially dependent on you at the time of your death.

Legal lore

This discrimination against same-sex partners is surely overdue for reform. In the leading case on the application of the Inheritance (etc) Act 1975 to same-sex partners, Lord Justice Ward stated, 'No distinction can sensibly be drawn between the two couples in terms of love, nurturing, fidelity, durability, emotional and economic interdependence – to make but some, and by no means all, of the hallmarks of a relationship between a husband and wife'.

Is there a proper legal term for a partner to whom one is not married?

The word *partner* is ambiguous, because it might mean a business associate as well as a cohabitee. If you want to leave something to your partner, name them so there is no doubt who you have in mind.

I wish to make a lot of small gifts of possessions that have sentimental value. Can I do this in a letter instead of in my will?

The answer is no, unless you refer to the letter in your will and give your executors the power to hand out the gifts in accordance with your letter. But be careful; the letter itself has no force in law. The safest option is always to make the gifts in the will.

—I'd like to leave my car to my nephew. But what if I change my car before I die? And what if I don't have a car at all when I die?

This is a common problem with what are called specific legacies (see *Buzzwords*). Remember that your will 'speaks from death'. You can't leave what you don't own. If you do not own the asset at the time of your death, the gift will fail. And if you own more than one car when you die, there will be an argument about who gets which car. And what happens if the car is on HP? For these reasons, a specific legacy of an asset such as a car, which you may change regularly, can be problematic. Consider giving a sum of money instead, otherwise use the Gift of Mutable Asset clause as shown on page 133.

—I prefer my cats to most people and I want to leave my fortune to the Cats' Protection League. I know my family won't like it and I am afraid that if they get their hands on the will they'll try to stop it. What can I do?

There are two precautions you can take. First, appoint professional executors, such as solicitors, and lodge your will with them. Second, send the charity a copy of your will so they know they should benefit when you die.

Legal lore

The major charities read through all wills that go through probate registries, searching for legacies. Every year they pick up on hundreds of legacies which unscrupulous families would otherwise try to keep for themselves.

Does a will have to be in English to be valid under UK law?

No, but it must still comply with UK law. Just because you write your will in Bengali, Islamic law will not apply!

Do I have to write my will on paper, or would an electronic version do?

No. The electronic version will be insufficient because the law does not yet recognise electronic signatures. As for writing the will on something other than paper, there is a famous case of a will written on the inside of an eggshell that was found to be valid. Don't risk it, however.

Who will own my body after I die?

This question is of more than academic interest in the context of recent scandals concerning the unauthorised removal and retention of body parts by hospitals. Nobody *owns* the body (which means that nobody has the right to sell it for spares). However, *possession* of the body passes to your executors or next of kin.

– I have a villa in Spain – can I leave it to someone in my will?

No, you cannot give your Spanish villa to anyone in a will made outside Spain. You should take advice from a Spanish lawyer. The likely result is that you will need two wills – one for your assets in the UK and a separate one for the villa. Note also that Spain, like several other countries, has 'forced heirship' laws that restrict your freedom to give what you want to whom you want (see *Offshore assets* on page 41).

If you do find yourself making two wills, take care over how they interact. First, you should specify in each will the assets to which it applies; second, you should ensure that the later of your two wills does not cancel the earlier one by an unqualified revocation (see *Buzzwords*) of all previous wills.

– I have been working in the UK on a long-term contract, but eventually my employer will want me back home. Can I make a will over here?

The key issue here is what is called 'domicile', that is, the country you call home (as distinct from your 'country of residence', which is where you happen to be living at the time). If you are not domiciled in England and Wales, you should not make a will without taking advice from a lawyer in your home country. If you own real estate over here, you will have to make a will over here even if you need a second will to deal with assets elsewhere.

A foreign domicile has distinct advantages for Inheritance Tax (see page 32) purposes.

I own a timeshare – a week in Marbella. Can I leave it in my will?

It depends on the legal set-up. The critical distinction is between moveable property on the one hand and immoveable (ie real estate) on the other. A timeshare can fall into either category. In general, moveable property worldwide can be given in your will, but not immoveable property.

Take professional advice from someone with expertise in timeshares within the jurisdiction of your timeshare property (in this instance Spain).

Even if an annual week in Marbella is exactly what your intended recipient has always wanted, will they be able to afford the flights to get there? Additionally, there is the annual service and maintenance charge to consider. Can your intended beneficiary afford to take on this responsibility? They could of course sell the timeshare, but this too would give them trouble and expense.

Discuss your intentions with the proposed recipient first, because a timeshare can be something of a white elephant (see *Legal lore* below). A legacy of money might be more acceptable

Legal lore

White elephants

If you annoyed the King of Siam he might chop off your head; or, if he *really* had a down on you, he quietly ruined you by presenting you with a sacred white elephant. You had to accept the gift, you had to look after it, and you could not quietly slaughter it for steaks and elephant hide sofas.

—What happens to my debts when I die? Do they die with me?

You should be so lucky! But you can (at a price) take out insurance that will pay off specific debts – such as your mortgage and catalogue debts.

—What happens if my partner and I both die at the same time, for example in a car crash?

In practice, simultaneous death is rare. If you and your partner die together in an accident and it is impossible to determine which of you died first, the law will presume that whichever of you is older will have died first.

—I am getting a bit forgetful in my old age. Although I want to write a will, and know what I want to do with my estate, I am afraid that certain members of my family will challenge the will on the basis that I have lost my marbles. Help!

Have no fear! Ask your friendly GP to write a note saying that he/she has examined you and that you have 'testamentary capacity' (see *Buzzwords*). Put a copy of the note with your will (and consider disinheriting those who put you to this trouble and expense).

How much are you worth?

Before you make a will, make a list!

Here are four good reasons for doing so.

- You can really only give proper consideration to who should get what if you have taken the trouble to work out what you own.
- If there is a significant shortfall between your financial obligations and your means, you may want to consider ways of making up the difference (such as life insurance).
- You can find out whether your estate might be liable for Inheritance Tax, and do some forward planning to minimise that liability.
- You can provide your executors with a useful summary of what you have.

But how much will you be worth dead?

Take care. There may be significant differences between what you are worth in your lifetime and what you will be worth after you die. Consider

- *who dies first?* – if you have a spouse or partner, the one who dies last may well have twice as much to leave as the first one to die

- *joint property*, that is, property that you co-own with one or more other people. Remember that you only own your share
- *encumbered property* – that is, property subject to mortgages or other secured loans – you can count only the net value because the bank or building society will want paying back
- *insurance policies in trust* – the proceeds of the policy belong not to you, even though you pay the premiums, but to the person named in the policy as beneficiary.

Now take stock of everything you own – your *assets* – such as

- real estate (such as your home, land, etc.)
- contents
- cars
- bank and building society deposits
- Premium Bonds and other forms of national savings
- other investments, such as shares
- proceeds of life insurance policies
- pension and/or death-in-service entitlements
- works of art and antiques
- business assets
- tools and machinery
- jewellery
- other.

Try to work out the approximate value of what you own.

The total of all these headings will be your *gross estate.*

Now list *everything you owe* – your *liabilities* – such as

- mortgages
- loans and overdrafts
- hire purchase
- credit card debts
- catalogue debts
- other debts
- contingent liabilities – e.g. guarantees given for the debts of other people

Try to work out approximately how much you owe.

Your *net estate* is the difference between what you own and what you owe.

In simple terms

ASSETS – LIABILITIES = NET ESTATE

If you have a spouse or partner, you will find it helpful to consider separately the net estate of the first to die and the second to die.

Now make another list!

This is a list of people, not possessions. Think of everyone whom you ought to provide for in your will – give particular thought to people whom you would rather not provide for, but to whom you may have a legal obligation (see *Dependants* on page 59).

Inheritance Tax

You may think that only rich folks need to read this bit; and in general you would be right. But have a care! 'Rich' – in this context at least – means that you and your partner have net assets worth, in the 2001/2002 tax year, more than £242,000. With soaring property prices, quite a modest family home in a desirable location could be worth serious money and therefore attract Inheritance Tax.

What is it a tax on?

Inheritance Tax is a misleading name. It is NOT a tax on inheriting. It is a tax on dying with what the Inland Revenue classes as too much money, and the tax is charged on your estate. In theory it is possible to avoid or reduce the tax liability by reducing the value of your estate. In practice, this is often difficult to achieve because you may only be able to avoid the tax by giving away your home in your lifetime or giving away the savings that are important to your income.

When does Inheritance Tax NOT apply?

There is no Inheritance Tax payable on death in respect of

- gifts between husband and wife
- gifts to charity
- lifetime gifts made at least seven years before your death
- some small lifetime gifts – as long as the combined value of your gifts in any tax year (6 April to 5 April) is not more than £3,000 in total. So if you have a spouse or partner you can of course *each* give away up to £3,000
- lifetime gifts made from your income
- lifetime gifts on marriage.

And there is no Inheritance Tax payable on certain assets, notably

- business assets
- farm land.

But the rules relating to exempt assets are complex and if you think this involves you, take professional advice.

When does Inheritance Tax apply?

Subject to the exceptions mentioned above, the general rule is that Inheritance Tax is payable on the net value of your estate so far as it exceeds what is known as the *nil rate band.*

In the tax year 2001/2002, the nil rate band is £242,000 and the rate of Inheritance Tax is 40%. So, if the net value of your estate is £242,000 (or less), there is no tax to pay.

If the net value of your estate is £252,000, however, there will be tax to pay at 40% on £10,000 – ie Inheritance Tax of £4,000 on the part of your estate which is above the nil rate band line.

The example below shows how it works.

Estate	£252,000
Less	£242,000 nil rate band
Taxable estate	£10,000
Tax	£4,000

Note that in adding up the value of your estate for Inheritance Tax purposes, you must include

- your share of joint assets (whether or not you can leave them in your will (see page 41)
- the value of insurance policies (except policies written in trust, (see page 42) and
- the value of gifts that you make in the seven years before you die, *except* gifts of under £3,000 in any tax year and gifts from income.

Who pays Inheritance Tax?

The obligation to pay Inheritance Tax lies with the executors. They pay the tax using money they raise from your estate. Usually the tax is paid out of the *residue* of your estate (see *Buzzwords*), unless the residue is not enough, or unless you state otherwise in your will.

Think carefully. Is it fair on the residuary beneficiary – that is, the person inheriting what is left over after the specific legacies (see *Buzzwords*) have been distributed – to be lumbered with all the tax?

Beware – there are two traps with lifetime gifts.

1. The nil rate band of Inheritance Tax is applied to gifts in the chronological order in which you make them. This means that substantial lifetime gifts will reduce the amount of your estate on death which will benefit from the nil rate band. So generosity in your lifetime may, if you don't live on for seven years, penalise the people you meant to benefit in your will.

2. The recipient of any potentially tax-exempt lifetime gift is primarily liable for the tax on the value of the gift. Of course, the nil rate band may come to the rescue, but if it has already been used up, it can't! In that case the recipient will have to pay – unless your will provides otherwise (an outcome which you may or may not desire). The precedent wills in this book provide that any tax will be paid from the residuary (see *Buzzwords*) estate, to the extent that there is enough money in the kitty.

Common Inheritance Tax avoidance strategies

There are three features of Inheritance Tax that provide opportunities for avoidance (which is legal – as opposed to evasion, which is not):

1. Lifetime and death gifts between husband and wife (but not unmarried partners) are free of Inheritance Tax.

2. Inheritance Tax is not payable on (nearly all) lifetime gifts made at least seven years before you die. If you die within the seven years, the value of the lifetime gift is added back into the value of your estate for the purpose of calculating Inheritance Tax liability. But the amount of tax on the lifetime gift reduces on a sliding scale – the further you survive into the seven-year period, the less tax is payable.

3. Inheritance Tax on death is not payable on the value (currently £242,000) of the nil rate band. Everyone can therefore, at current banding levels, leave £242,000 free of tax.

So to avoid tax ...

- Make lifetime gifts and live another seven years – but take care.
- Lifetime gifts to your spouse will not save Inheritance Tax because they're exempt anyway (see above) – although they can be useful to equalise assets (see below).
- Some lifetime gifts may attract Capital Gains Tax, so in avoiding Scylla you may founder on Charybdis.
- If you have a long-term partner but are not married, consider marriage to take advantage of the inter-spouse exemption!
- If you are married or have a partner, consider arranging your affairs to make use of *both* your nil rate bands – thereby increasing the maximum you can leave free of tax from £242,000 to £484,000 (at current rates). There are two stages to this:
    1. Seek to avoid the 'bunching' of assets in the name of one partner/spouse. You cannot make maximum use of your nil rate band unless you own assets of that value.
    2. Write your will to give as much as you can afford to non-exempt beneficiaries – such as children – up to the limit of the nil rate band (currently £242,000); but without going over the top.
- And finally, your 'last will and testament' need not be the *last word*! After you die, your executors and adult beneficiaries are allowed to rewrite your will – so far as it does not affect the share of any beneficiary

who is under 18 or who is unable or unwilling to give informed consent to the changes. This facility can be used to improve the tax efficiency of your will, but for this purpose the changes must be made within two years of your death and notified to the Inland Revenue. If your executors/beneficiaries are minded to do this, they should take professional advice.

Keep tax saving in proportion

Even if you *are* rich enough to worry about Inheritance Tax, do try to keep a sense of proportion about your tax liability. Don't beggar yourself, or someone you love, for a small tax saving.

Tax is a complicated and ever-changing subject

This book is not a definitive guide to Inheritance Tax planning. If you think your estate may come into the Inheritance Tax bracket, and if tax planning is important to you, take advice from a professional.

The people who have most difficulty with Inheritance Tax are those with assets that only modestly exceed the nil rate band, because they are vulnerable to the tax but not wealthy enough to give a lot away and still have enough on which to live. These people have the most to gain from more esoteric tax saving strategies, such as discretionary trusts (see *Buzzwords*).

Financial planning – how to be worth more dead than alive

Will your net estate after you die be enough to

- pay your debts, such as your mortgage?
- take care of your children until they can take care of themselves?
- support your partner or other dependants?

Of course, there never seems to be enough money to go round, but at least with life insurance you can make sure you are worth more dead than alive. Bear in mind that there are three types of life insurance. These are, in order of cost:

- *term insurance:* this insures your life for a fixed period of time, at the end of which you do not receive any return on your money;
- *whole-life insurance:* this pays out when you die (whenever that is);
- *endowment insurance:* this pays out when you die, or at the end of a fixed period of time, whichever is earlier.

Bear in mind that whole-life and endowment insurances are in effect combined insurance and investment products. The problem is one of *transparency*: the return that you get on the policy may not reflect the underlying performance of the assets that the insurer holds on your behalf. In bad times, this may benefit you, because the insurers do not deduct investment losses from the value of your policy (believe us, they would if they were allowed to!). But in good times it means they may not be passing on the profits they make on your money.

From whom do you buy insurance? There are two types of salesman. One is a 'tied agent' who will only offer the products of one insurance company. The other is an 'independent financial adviser'. But most people selling insurance, independent or otherwise, are on commission. Is the policy the salesman is pushing by any chance the one which gets him the juiciest cut?

Life insurance can also be used for Inheritance Tax planning (see page 34). The financial services industry also sells sophisticated trust schemes that enable older people to give away capital and have enough income to live on at the same time.

Do get the right advice. Go to an independent financial adviser, and shop around. There are websites that will help you to do this.

Can you leave it in your will?

Offshore assets

If you have assets abroad, you may not be able to give them away in a will made in England and Wales. For example, some countries have 'forced heirship' laws which dictate who is allowed to inherit the assets that you own in their jurisdiction.

You may also need to make more than one will – that is, one for each jurisdiction where you have assets. In this event, take care over how the two wills interact. First, you should specify in each will the assets to which it applies; second, you should ensure that the later of your two wills does not cancel the earlier one by an unqualified revocation (see *Buzzwords*) of all previous wills.

If you think this applies to you, seek professional advice.

Jointly owned property

The commonest example is the family home that you own jointly with your spouse or partner. But the same principle applies to all jointly owned assets, such as shares, bank and building society accounts, house contents, etc.

You cannot give in your will your share of joint assets that you own on the basis that if one joint owner dies, their share passes automatically to the survivor(s). This is called the rule of survivorship, and applies unless you do something about it before you die. If this means you, see *Joint property – tying up the loose ends* on page 101.

Legal lore

Where the rule of survivorship applies, lawyers say that you own the asset as *joint tenant* with the other owner(s). Where you can leave your share of the asset in your will, you are said to own it as a *tenant in common*. The phrases have nothing to do with paying rent to a landlord and everything to do with the Latin *tenere* – to hold or own.

Insurance policies written in trust

You may be paying into an insurance policy for the benefit of a partner or child. If you die, the proceeds of that policy belong to the person(s) named in it as beneficiaries. So the money is not yours to give away in your will. When you die, the money will go direct to that person.

This type of insurance policy can be a useful tax planning device because the proceeds do not count as part of your estate.

Pension and death in service benefits

Pension schemes will often automatically pay out a reduced pension for your widow or widower. If you are not married, you may be able to nominate a long-term partner to receive the pension instead. The amount of the pension (if any), and its recipient, are at the discretion of the trustees of your pension fund, and for that reason will not form part of your estate for tax purposes. The trustees are likely to take account of your wishes.

If you die in harness, your pension fund may pay a lump sum to your widow or widower. Again, if you are not married you may be able to nominate who is to receive it. The payment will not form part of your estate for tax purposes, as it is discretionary. As a lot of money may be involved, it is well worth finding out how much may be available and what you should do to make sure it goes to whom you want.

Rented property

Of course, if you do not own your home, you cannot leave it to anyone in your will.

But, if you are the tenant of a rented home that you share with other people, you should consider ensuring they have somewhere to live after you die. You may be able to pass on the *tenancy*, although the right to do so is much less available to tenancies granted after

15 January 1989. The precise legal position depends on who is your landlord, and when your tenancy was granted.

Legal lore

The significance of 15 January 1989 is that it is the date when the old Rent Acts went out and the new Housing Act came in. Tenancies granted before 15 January 1989 come under a different set of rules from those granted after that date.

- *Private sector landlord; tenancy granted before 15 January 1989*. The likelihood is that there will be a statutory right of succession (see *Buzzwords*) to the tenancy after your death. If you were the original tenant, your spouse or partner living with you when you die will be entitled to a new tenancy on the same statutory basis as your old tenancy. Another member of your family who lived with you for two years before your death will also be entitled to a new tenancy, although the terms will, particularly regarding rent, be less favourable. There is also a limited right to a second succession. If in doubt, seek professional advice.
- *Private sector landlord; tenancy granted on or after 15 January 1989*. There is no statutory succession unless this tenancy is the successor to one granted before 15 January 1989 (see above).
- *Council tenancy*. Unless the accommodation is on a short-term, temporary basis, the tenancy will be a 'secure tenancy' that can be 'inherited' by members

of your family. If you were the original tenant, your spouse living with you when you die is entitled to 'inherit' the tenancy. Other members of your family, including your (unmarried) partner, may be entitled to 'inherit' the tenancy if they were living with you for 12 months before your death. But there are restrictions. The tenancy cannot be 'inherited' if you are the sole tenant and were previously a joint tenant or have yourself 'inherited' the tenancy.

- *Housing association tenancy granted before 15 January 1989*. The legal rights of successors are the same as for Council tenants.
- *Housing association tenancy granted on or after 15 January 1989*. The position of successors is the same as for the tenants of private landlords, except in certain transitional cases.

In practice, you need to clarify the position with your landlord in your lifetime so that any family living with you will know whether they will have security of tenure after you die. If in doubt, seek legal advice.

Who gets what?

In deciding who gets what, you may want to treat all your beneficiaries (see *Buzzwords*) equally, or take into account

- gifts you have already made
- the differing future needs of people close to you.

If you are married or living with someone, you should give careful consideration to the future of your partner. Make sure they've got enough to live on after your death.

Typical ways of providing for those you care about are set out in the will forms included in this book and on the website. These are

- everything to your partner*
- everything to your children
- everything to your partner, but if your partner dies first, everything to your children
- everything to your partner, but if your partner dies first, everything to other beneficiaries or charity
- everything to charity.

---

*This includes husbands, wives and live-in lovers. And we offer a version of *Will 1* (see page 105) that is suitable for same-sex partners.

You can also add legacies of money or possessions – we show you how.

KISS

The golden rule is – *K*eep *I*t *S*eriously *S*imple! – KISS.

The more complicated your will, the more likely you are to slip up. If you want to do something fancy, consult the website; and if that does not offer what you want, seek professional advice.

Executors

Your executors (see *Buzzwords*) will sort out your affairs after your death. But whom should you choose? Bear in mind that your executor will be in a position of responsibility. An executor has always had a duty to exercise reasonable skill and care. Since 1 February 2001, however, executors have also had a statutory duty of care in carrying out certain functions, such as

- making investments
- arranging insurance
- delegating tasks.

An executor who causes financial loss to your estate through failure to exercise skill and care can be sued by your beneficiaries. You can write your will to modify or exclude these statutory duties, but whether it is sensible to do so is another matter.

You should NOT appoint

- people under the age of 18
- people who will not be able to cope – although bear in mind that they can of course get professional help (at a price)
- people you do not trust
- people who live too far away or are too busy.

You do not *need* to appoint a professional executor, such as a solicitor or a bank, but it may be sensible to do so if there is no one in your family willing or able to take on the duty of care (see above). There may be compelling reasons to appoint a professional if

- the family would otherwise be at each other's throats
- your affairs are complicated
- the terms of your will impose long-term responsibilities on your executors/trustees.

But beware – the professionals won't do it for free and once you are dead they are difficult to get rid of. Banks tend to be more expensive than solicitors – try to get an indication of what they will charge.

How many executors?

You can appoint as many executors as you like, but only the first four will be allowed to take out the grant of probate (see *Buzzwords)*. Although this is something of a rarity, you can have additional executors for particular assets, such as a literary executor to protect your intellectual property rights on the books you have had published.

If everything is going to your spouse or partner, it may be sensible to make them your sole executor. Otherwise, two is the ideal number of executors. You will often need two anyway, to deal with any 'real estate' (see *Buzzwords*). Also, one executor can keep an eye on the other. Consider appointing a substitute executor – like an understudy in the theatre – who can take the place of someone who, when you die, is unable or unwilling to act.

Don't give someone a nasty shock when you die! If you want to appoint someone as your executor, ask them first (although legally you don't need to do so). The following is a sample letter asking someone to be your executor.

> *Dear*
>
> *I shall shortly be making my Will and I should very much like to name you as one of my executors, together with [name]. You and [name] would be responsible for carrying out the instructions in my Will. You would have a duty to exercise reasonable skill and care in doing so. Your out of pocket expenses would of course be paid, but you would not be paid for your time.*
>
> *Could you please let me know if you are willing to take this on?*
>
> *Yours ever,*

Guardians

Victorian novels often have orphans and the guardians who had total control over their lives. The guardian took on the powers and responsibilities of the child's dead parents.

The basic function of a guardian remains the same today, but the legal framework has evolved and is now on a statutory basis under the Children Act 1989. Under the Act, the child's interests are paramount.

What does a guardian do?

A guardian takes on parental responsibility (see *Buzzwords*) for a child and cares for the child when there is no parent to do so. This is why forms giving written permission for a child to go on a school trip or to have an operation have to be signed by a 'Parent or Guardian'.

Who can appoint a guardian?

A parent with parental responsibility for a child under 18 (including an adopted or illegitimate child) may appoint a guardian for that child.

- *The mother* of a child automatically has parental responsibility, irrespective of marital status.
- *The father* will have automatic parental responsibility *if he was married to the mother at the time of the child's birth.*

- But otherwise the father will not normally have parental responsibility unless he applies to a court for it or the mother grants it using the official form.

A guardian may also be appointed by the court (as in *a ward of court*).

—When does the appointment of a guardian take effect?

The guardian will take over after you die if the other parent is also dead. The guardian can also take over if the other parent is still alive when you die provided *either* at that time the child has been living with you under a residence order, *or* the other parent does not have parental responsibility.

—How is a guardian appointed?

In practice, it is convenient to do this in your will (see *Will 2* on page 110). In theory, it can also be done in a separate document as long as it is signed in the presence of two witnesses, and dated.

Appointing guardians is particularly important to unmarried mothers because the child's father does not automatically have parental responsibility (see above).

Ask before you appoint!

Your children's guardian will have parental responsibility (see *Buzzwords*) for them until they reach 18. This can place a big personal and financial burden on the guardian, so you need to make sure the potential guardian agrees in advance to take it on.

Finance for guardians

You should if possible leave some money in your will for your children's needs, and/or consider buying yourself some life insurance cover (see page 39).

But there is help on offer. Broadly, in handing out benefits and making tax allowances, officialdom makes little distinction between a child in the care of a guardian and the guardian's own children.

Child benefit: If the child lives with the guardian, the guardian will qualify for the ordinary, non-means-tested child benefit just as a natural parent would. The rates as of April 2001 are £15.50 per week for the first child and £10.35 for the second child and subsequent children. Contact the local Benefits Agency office (details in the local telephone directory) in the first instance.

Guardian's allowance: This is a non-means-tested weekly payment which guardians can claim in addition to child benefit. As of April 2001 the weekly rate is £9.70 for the first child and £11.35 for the second child and subsequent children. To claim it, the guardian needs a Form BG1. For advice and information, contact the local Benefits Agency office (details in the local telephone directory). There is also a special Guardian's Allowance Unit (details in *Useful Contacts*).

Income Support/Family Credit: Guardians receiving either of these means-tested benefits can claim for the children in their care just as a natural parent would.

Tax relief: A guardian can also claim the usual allowances against income tax. Your local Inland Revenue office will advise on your individual case.

Child maintenance will usually continue after your death and be passed on to the child's guardian. Any court order for child maintenance will remain in force and the money will be paid to the guardian for the child's benefit. If an absent parent is paying child support through the Child Support Agency at the time of your death, the order will lapse. BUT the guardian can immediately make a fresh claim as if they were the parent.

Gifts to children in your will

The law assumes that children under 18 cannot be trusted with money. So your executors cannot hand money direct to children who are under 18 when you die. Your will should therefore provide a way for your executors to pay over the money or look after it for the children. This can be done in two ways:

- The will provides for an adult to give the executors a receipt for the money;
- The executors as trustees hold the money in trust until the child reaches 18, or whatever higher age you specify, up to age 25. Any older than 25 would normally pose tax problems. You can specify that in the meantime the capital or income can be used for the child's education or maintenance.

Children with learning disabilities may need to be treated differently (see page 95).

In practice, use the first option for small gifts, and the second option for larger ones.

Points to consider

- Is it possible that you might have more children before you die? Remember that both men and women can now have children at advanced ages. Leave your options open in your will by referring to 'my children' rather than naming them individually.
- If you have children under 18, you may want to appoint guardians (see page 51).
- If you have a child with special needs, see page 95.
- The gifts in our standard will are expressed as 'age contingent' – that is, the child receives the money only if they live to that age. Despite this, the income – and indeed the capital – can still be used for this child's maintenance and education in the meantime.
- There may be a tax penalty to an 'age contingent' gift, because trustees pay a higher rate of income tax. This rate is known as the RAT – Rate Applicable to Trusts – and in 2001 is 34%, except for dividend income, which is taxed at 25%.

Tax is payable on *all* the income from the trust because trustees cannot take advantage of the child's personal tax allowance. You can have it both ways, however, by giving the income to the child or using it for the child's benefit, such as to pay school fees; but the trustees may still find it time-consuming to recover the tax. This is explained in leaflet IR152, available on the Inland Revenue's website >inlandrevenue.gov.uk<. Trusts are not a DIY matter, however; seek professional advice.

- An age-contingent gift begs the question of the age at which the gift is made over to (or 'vests in') the child. There are two considerations. First, there are tax disadvantages if the 'vesting age' is over 25. Second, the law ('the rule against perpetuities') forbids overlong delays before the gift is handed over. In practice, the 'vesting age' for grandchildren should not exceed 21 unless you are *certain* that no more will be born after you die, who could benefit from your gift. This is a complex area of the law. If in doubt, seek professional advice.
- An age-contingent gift will generate income (you hope!). This income can be added to the original capital, but this process – 'accumulation' – is not allowed to go on for more than 21 years.

Legal lore

The rule against accumulation came about as a result of the will of a fabulously rich merchant named Peter Thellusson (1737-97). He directed that the income from his fortune should be added to the capital for the lifetimes of his children, grandchildren and great-grandchildren. The government of the day did some arithmetic and realised that by the end of this period the Thellusson heirs would own the entire country (this was before the days of Bill Gates). So they passed the Accumulations Act 1800 to prevent this disaster. Various members of the Thellusson family then spent 60 years arguing in the courts about who should get what.

The dispute was a model for the long-running case of *Jarndyce* v *Jarndyce* in Dickens's *Bleak House.*

- In the case of an outright gift to a child under 18, your will must provide for someone else to give the executors a receipt for the money, because the child cannot do so.
- In the form we use, all your children – legitimate, illegitimate or adopted – are equal under your will BUT a child whom you treat as your own, but of whom you are not the parent, such as a stepchild, will not benefit automatically. You should make special provision for such children, mentioning them by name.

'Class Gifts' – including grandchildren

Gifts to a particular group ('my grandchildren', 'my colleagues at Bloggs's Bacon Factory') are known as *class gifts*. There are two common problems with these. The first is to identify who exactly comes into the class. If it is not possible to do this (for example, do you mean people who worked in the factory at the time that you made your will, or at the time of your death, and what does 'colleague' really mean?) the gift will, as the lawyers say, 'fail for uncertainty'.

The second problem is to name a cut-off date after which nobody new can join the club. A common example is grandchildren (how can you predict whether any will be born after your death?) and the usual fix is to restrict the gift to 'all my grandchildren living at the time of my death'.

Dependants – especially the ones you'd prefer to disinherit!

The Inheritance (etc) Act states that if you die without making reasonable financial provision for your family and dependants, they can make a claim on your estate. And 'dependants' *include*

- your spouse
- your dependent children
- a 'child of the family' – ie a stepchild
- your ex-spouse, unless they have remarried or a court order has excluded their rights under the Act – see below
- your (opposite-sex) partner if you have been living together for at least two years before your death
- any other person who immediately before your death was being maintained by you (this may include a carer).

Dependants (unless they come within the final category of the list above) *exclude*

- same-sex partners, however long you have been together
- children of a partner to whom you are not married.

If you want to exclude a dependant from your will, take legal advice. You cannot defeat a dependant's claim under the Act by making a pre-emptive lifetime gift to

someone else unless you live on for six years after making the gift.

—**1.** If you are divorced, or in the process of divorcing, you can get a court order to bar your spouse or ex-spouse from making a claim against your estate. This is common practice in an order for financial provision on divorce, especially when the order is made by consent. An order can also be obtained where there is a judicial separation or an annulment. If you believe this may apply to you, seek legal advice.

—**2.** If you want to exclude someone from your will who you think would then be able to make an Inheritance (etc) Act claim, you should make what is called a 'Section 21 statement'. That is, you make a written statement either in or enclosed with your will that explains your reasons for excluding that person. A good reason for excluding them might be that you had already provided for their future during your lifetime. A less good reason, but one which often arises, is that the potential claimant would lose out on state benefits if you left them any significant amount of money (in such circumstances, consider a discretionary trust).

Legal lore

For technical reasons, Section 21 of the Inheritance etc Act was repealed in 1995, but the spirit of Section 21 statements lives on. If you think there may be a potential claim against your estate, and a Section 21statement will help, you can and should still make one.

Marriage and divorce

Marriage automatically cancels any will made before the marriage, unless it is clearly made with that marriage in mind.

Legal lore

In 1837 Parliament was afraid that a man (it was nearly always a man) on his way to the altar might be so preoccupied that he might forget to alter his will; and his bride might then lose out. So they passed the Wills Act 1837, which provided that marriage revoked any previous will and his widow would inherit.

BUT if he made a will after the marriage (or before it, with that marriage in mind), the law did not interfere, even if the wife was left out. In 1837 it was considered improper to interfere with a man's right to dispose of his property as he wished. Nowadays, of course, hard-done-by widows and widowers can usually claim under the Inheritance (etc) Act (see above).

If you do wish to make a will with a forthcoming marriage in mind, there are forms of words that will make your intentions clear. These can be found on page 135.

- If you get divorced – that is, if the court makes a decree absolute – your former spouse is cut out of the will, both as beneficiary and executor. But the rest of the will takes effect in the usual way. Remember – unless a court order is in place (see page 60), the ex-spouse may still be able to make a claim under the Inheritance (etc) Act.

Don't delay, act today!

If your marriage breaks down irretrievably (this is the word the law uses) you should immediately make a new will.

- Don't wait for the decree absolute.
- Don't just cancel or destroy your old will – the intestacy rules (see *Buzzwords*) will work in your estranged spouse's favour.
- If you die in the interim, your spouse, *who is still legally married to you,* will inherit as if you were still together.

Second time around

Consider the situation where you have children from your first marriage, and you have now remarried (congratulations, you now have a 'blended family'). You will want to make proper financial provision for the children of your first marriage, and also for your new spouse and any children you may have together. There is potential for conflict between the interests of your two families. There is no easy solution unless you have 'loadsa' money.

In this situation it is vital that you do make a will (think of the potential claims under the Inheritance (etc) Act.) Seek legal advice.

Funeral arrangements

'Let's talk of graves, of worms and epitaphs.'
Shakespeare, *Richard II*.

You do not have to include your funeral arrangements in your will, and there may be good reasons not to do so:

- If nobody reads your will until after your funeral, your wishes may be overlooked.
- Your executors are not bound by your funeral instructions, and in fact they have the legal power to cremate your body whatever your stated preference (it is of course open to you to come back and haunt them).

The variety of funeral arrangements you ask for is infinite, but have a care about practicality and expense.

Pre-paid funerals

One way that may ensure your wishes are carried out is to arrange and pay for your funeral in advance. Many funeral directors offer this service. But beware:

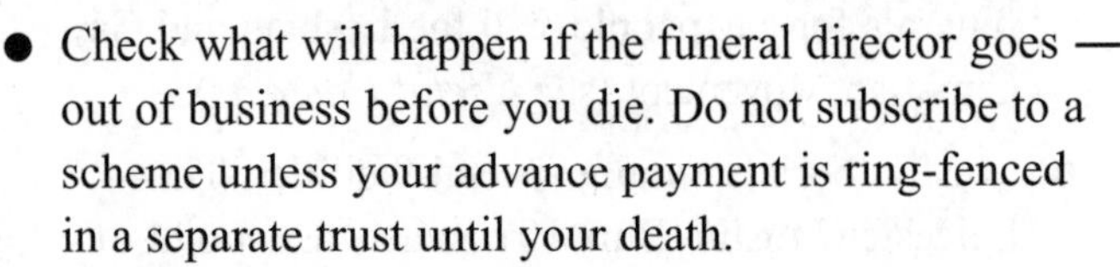

- Check what will happen if the funeral director goes out of business before you die. Do not subscribe to a scheme unless your advance payment is ring-fenced in a separate trust until your death.
- If you intend to pay by instalments, check what will

happen if you die before the final payment (you can usually take out payment protection insurance).

- Check what will happen if you die out of the funeral director's area.
- Make sure your family know about the arrangement, because there may not be a refund – keep a copy of the paperwork with your will.

Ask around your local funeral directors if this idea appeals to you.

What kind of funeral?

Detailed advice on funeral arrangements is outside the scope of this book, but here are a few sources of inspiration.

- For information about non-religious ceremonies, contact the British Humanist Association. It offers a free booklet entitled *To Celebrate a Life* and will supply a list of people in your area who can conduct non-religious ceremonies (see *Useful Contacts*).
- For information about green burials and a list of sites in your area, contact the Natural Death Centre (see *Useful Contacts*).
- For a list of priests happy to conduct Christian funerals for gay people, call the Lesbian and Gay Christian Movement (see *Useful Contacts*).
- Muslim burials require special facilities. The Leicester Muslim Burial Trust acts as a point of contact for Muslim funerals throughout the UK and

offers a seven-days a week helpline (see *Useful Contacts*).

Can you DIY?

Many grieving families prefer to hand over the funeral arrangements to a professional. A funeral director will take care of everything – at a price.

However, you do *not* need to engage professional funeral directors, and the saving if your family arrange a DIY funeral can be substantial. For further details see the *New Natural Death Handbook* (details in *Useful Contacts*) which discusses everything from budget-price coffins to the ceremony itself.

Burial on private land

> **'We buried him darkly at dead of night.' Charles Wolfe, *The Burial of Sir John Moore at Corunna***

You do not have to have your body buried in an official burial ground. A single burial in your back garden (provided it is *your* garden and not your landlord's) does not usually require official permission, but it *may* do so. The current legal position seems to be that a single burial in an unmarked grave (though an apple tree would not count as 'marking') does not require planning permission, but monumental masonry or fencing may do so, since they are forms of 'development'.

Furthermore, multiple burials on the same site may require planning permission for change of use of the land. Your burial should not disturb an archaeological site without permission. You may also require permission from the water authority if the burial threatens to pollute the water supply and the landowner's permission if you yourself do not own the site. If you die of a virulent disease, a burial on private land may be undesirable for reasons of public health or waste management.

In some places there are regulations about the depth of graves.

After the burial, the date and place must be notified within 96 hours to the Registrar of Births, Marriages and Deaths on the form provided for the purpose.

To prevent surprises for future occupants of the property, we would also recommend that a plan showing the position of the grave should be placed with the title deeds of the property. The Land Registry does not require notification.

DIY cremation?

It depends what you mean by DIY...

Legal lore

William Price, a Welsh doctor and part time Druid, whimsically named his infant son Jesus Christ. The child died young, and Dr Price ritually burned the body on a

> funeral pyre. There was outrage in the valleys. Dr Price was prosecuted, but only to be acquitted when it became apparent that he had not broken the law. This resulted in the introduction of the Cremation Act 1902, which now regulates such activities and made it a criminal offence not to use an official crematorium.
>
> There have been no open-air cremations in the UK since the 1940s, when the body of a Nepalese diplomat was cremated on a funeral pyre on private land in southern England.

You can certainly arrange a cremation without using a funeral director, but you must use an official crematorium. Using a funeral pyre in the back garden, even on Guy Fawkes night, is a criminal offence under the Cremation Act.

Most religions allow cremation, except orthodox Judaism, Islam, Eastern Orthodox Christianity and a few Fundamentalist Christian faiths. The Roman Catholic Church accepts cremation 'as long as it is not chosen for reasons which are contrary to Christian teachings'. If this worries you, ask your priest for guidance.

For further information about cremation, see *A Consumer's Guide to Funerals* (details in *Useful contacts*).

Scattering ashes

If you want your ashes scattered on private land, whoever does the scattering will need the landowner's permission.

Burial at sea

The days are gone when the sailmaker sewed you up in canvas – putting the last stitch through your nose to make sure you were dead – and placed a cannon ball at your feet.

For burial at sea you now need a licence. This is issued free of charge by DEFRA (Department of the Environment, Farming and Rural Affairs). But that is the cheap, easy bit. Burial at sea is now regulated to prevent bodies getting washed up on bathing beaches and getting caught in fishing nets. There are now only three places around the coast where sea burials are allowed. One is nine miles off shore from the mouth of the River Tyne, and the other two are on the South Coast – one off Newhaven and the other off the Isle of Wight.

Medical use of your body after death

There are two ways in which your body can be used after you die. The first is donation of organs (your own organs, not someone else's!) for transplant purposes. The second is donation of your entire body for teaching and/or research.

Donating organs

'...Let my body help others to lead fuller lives.'
Robert Test.

You can choose to donate any part of your body that the doctors have a use for, or specify organs, such as kidneys, heart, liver, corneas, lungs or pancreas.

For organ donation, time is of the essence. The cornea is the only part of your body that can wait up to 12 hours. All other organs must be removed immediately after 'brain stem death' with machines keeping the blood circulating. Your body will therefore be past its sell by date by the time anyone reads such intentions in your will.

So, if you want to donate your organs

- register on the NHS Organ Donor Register (see the registration form reproduced below);
- carry a donor card. The Literature Line (see below) will send you one, or you can get one from any chemist's shop or doctor's surgery;
- tell your family and friends in advance that you wish to donate your organs.

The Organ Donor Literature Line (details in *Useful contacts*) will send information to help you to decide whether you wish to donate your organs, and if so, which organs.

No stamp required

The NHS Organ Donor Register,
P.O. Box 14,
FREEPOST
Patchway
BRISTOL
BS34 8ZZ

☐ Please register me on the NHS Organ Donor Register as someone whose organs can be used for transplantation after my death. FILL IN SECTIONS 1 & 2.

☐ Please amend my details held on the NHS Organ Donor Register. FILL IN SECTIONS 1 & 2 and 3 if applicable.

☐ Please remove my entry from the NHS Organ Donor Register as I no longer wish to be a donor. FILL IN SECTIONS 1 & 3 if applicable and in SECTION 2, tick box B and sign.

1. Your name and address

Surname

Forename(s)

Date of birth / / Male Female

Current address

Postcode

2. Your wishes

A. I request that after my death:- any part of my body ☐

or my:- Kidneys ☐ Heart ☐ Liver ☐ Corneas ☐

Lungs ☐ Pancreas ☐ may be used for the treatment of others.

B. I request that my name is removed from the NHS Organ Donor Register ☐

Signature

Date / /

3. Please tick if you're an existing donor ☐ and fill in your details below if your name or address has changed since you first registered.

Previous name

Previous address

Postcode

What to do next.
Post this form using the address overleaf. You don't need to use a stamp, but doing so helps conserve our funds. Thank you.

Donating your body

Medical teaching

'Why, pet, my body is only an old cornflake packet. If the bairns can learn something by cutting it up, good luck to them.' Tommy Border, 1982.

The Professor of Anatomy at the University of Cambridge, W. A. Harris, put it more gracefully in 2001:

The study of anatomy ...helps to lay the foundations for all future ... medical practice ...We recognise that the donation of a body may be a person's last act of benevolence reflecting a life of generosity, for which we are enormously grateful.

Bear in mind that once you have donated your body, it comes under the control of the medical school, with no conditions attached other than the choice of eventual burial or cremation. To offer to donate your body, you should contact the anatomy department at your nearest medical school. In the London area, the contact is the London Anatomy Office (details in *Useful contacts*). Otherwise call HM Inspector of Anatomy at the Department of Health (details in *Useful contacts*). They will usually send you an explanatory leaflet and their own form of authorisation, which allows for you to choose between burial and cremation after examination (otherwise use the example form on page 139).

There is no guarantee that your body will be accepted. Medical schools prefer bodies that are within easy collecting distance. Age does not matter, but the following disorders will usually disqualify a body:

- post mortem examination;
- removal of major organs for transplant purposes;
- an amputated limb;
- extensive surgery;
- obesity or emaciation;
- a history of cancer;
- Alzheimer's disease and some other neurological disorders;
- tuberculosis;
- hepatitis;
- gangrene;
- HIV/AIDS.

You will see from this list of 'disqualifications' that you cannot have it both ways – you cannot donate both your organs for transplant *and* your body for medical examination. What you can do, however, is leave instructions to your family that in the event of your organs not being removed for transplant for whatever reason, you wish your body to be donated for medical examination.

The procedure is simple. When you die your family must notify the medical school as soon as possible so that they can decide whether they can accept it. Your family must also notify the local Registrar of Births, Marriages and Deaths and obtain a Certificate for Burial or Cremation. Then, if your body is accepted, the medical school will send an undertaker (usually at their expense) to collect your body.

After that, there is usually no further communication between the medical school and your family and/or executors unless, at the time you make your donation, you ask for your ashes to be returned to your family.

Do bear in mind that if you donate your body for students to learn on, the medical school may need it for a long time. The legal maximum is three years. This will of course have implications for your funeral, due to the absence of a body. One answer is a service of thanksgiving shortly after your death.

A small group of students will be taught using the same body for the whole teaching year. At Cambridge there is a non-denominational committal service within the Anatomy Department. At this service the students and staff give thanks to those who have generously given their bodies to train the next generation of doctors. Professor Harris says, 'For the first time, during the committal service, the students learn the name of the person they have studied. This is important for our students and they are given time in which to say a personal and private "thank you"'. At some other medical schools, donors' families may be invited to the service: practices vary.

Medical research

If you want to donate your body for medical research rather than for students to dissect, this too is possible, although it is more of a loan than a donation (see below).

If you feel strongly about experiments on animals, you will be pleased to know that Peterborough District Hospital's Human Research Tissue Bank makes use of human tissue for testing drugs. The department will collect bodies from within a 150-mile radius. At mid-2001 there is no national tissue bank, although there are plans to set one up.

As with organ donation, time is of the essence, so it is important to register with the scheme during your lifetime – using, if you wish, the consent forms on its website (see *Useful Contacts*). They will then send you a laminated donor card with the hospital's details.

Bodies are kept for just 24 hours, after which they are returned to the family. There is a free information pack available, together with consent forms (see *Useful Contacts*).

Giving permission for use of your body for teaching or research

The doctors or scientists will not want to use your body unless they are confident that this is what you would have wanted. The clearest way to make your wishes known is to complete a form of authorisation that you should sign. The form also tells the doctors

- whether they can retain body parts and tissue after the examination, and
- what to do with your body afterwards.

We provide an example general form of authorisation on page 139 and on the website. You need to complete the form and sign it. After you have done so, keep the form with your will.

The Human Research Tissue Bank has its own form of authorisation (see above).

Living wills

All sick people are entitled to refuse treatment; and a doctor who persists in treating patients against their express instructions may be guilty of criminal assault. But what happens if you are incurably ill but no longer have the mental capacity to refuse treatment? The answer is to make your wishes known beforehand. An advance request of this kind is often called a living will.

A living will, therefore, is not really a will at all. It is a request not to be kept alive artificially when

- you are incurably ill
- your quality of life is very poor
- you no longer have the mental capacity to decide for yourself or to make your views known.

A living will does not yet have statutory force. All the same, the courts have in recent years determined that a living will, made in advance, which expresses your wishes clearly and is applicable to your case, will be as effective as a request made at the time. Additionally, the British Medical Association advises doctors that they are legally obliged to comply with such advance requests.

If you decide on a living will, make sure your family know about it, and send a copy to your GP.

Our book *Living Wills and Enduring Power of Attorney* in this series, gives you more information.

A living will/advance request should be kept separate from your will itself, otherwise nobody will know about it until it's too late. Always lodge copies with your doctor and your immediate family.

Making things easy for your executors

It is helpful if you can make a note of personal details that may be needed after your death – for example, the names and address of

- doctor
- Registrar of Births, Marriages and Deaths
- relations and friends
- employer
- bank
- building society
- accountant
- solicitor
- insurance broker
- landlord
- priest/minister/rabbi, etc.
- utilities, such as water, electricity and gas companies
- club, trade union, learned society or professional association.

It may be helpful to let your executors know where they can find your address book (either a paper version or a list on your PC), to enable them to call or write to anyone else who needs to know about your death.

It will also be helpful if you write down where your executors can find important documents, which might include

- birth certificate
- marriage certificate
- insurance policies
- pension documents
- title deeds to any property; or details of where to find these
- leases of property
- tenancy agreement and rent book
- hire purchase and loan agreements
- credit card and store card details
- building society and bank details
- Post Office savings account books
- copies of tax returns, etc
- passport
- receipts and guarantees for major purchases
- stocks and shares certificates
- National Insurance details
- vehicle registration documents and insurance details
- details of any liabilities which may not be immediately obvious to your executors, eg guarantees given for the debts of a company or individual.

Handing over the reins

Most of us hope to die at a ripe old age in full possession of our faculties.

Be realistic, however. If you are over 70 or in poor health, you should consider arranging for your affairs to be looked after by someone else if you become unable to deal with things for yourself.

The simplest way to do this is to make what is called an Enduring Power of Attorney (EPA for short). There is a special form for this – nothing else will do. An EPA gives the person of your choice – your attorney – the right to take over the running of your affairs in such circumstances. Otherwise, a person *not* of your choice – an official from the Public Guardianship Office will take over.

As soon as your attorney believes that you can no longer cope mentally, they have a duty to register your EPA with the Public Guardianship Office. The effect of registration is to give your attorney the power to continue to handle your affairs.

Details of the Public Guardianship Office are in *Useful contacts.*

Signing your will

Let us suppose you have taken all our advice and made your will. Congratulations – but it won't be legally binding until you sign it.

You need witnesses

Signing your will is one thing you *can't* do on your own. You need two adult, independent witnesses who are not

- beneficiaries or their partners
- executors or their partners
- members of your family
- under 18
- blind
- mentally incapable.

Two neighbours or work colleagues would be ideal witnesses, as long as you don't plan to leave them anything in your will.

Remember the witnesses are signing to say they have seen you sign your will. They do *not* need to know what is in your will.

How it's done

1. You sign your will first, in ink, at the very end of the will, with both witnesses watching. There is no need for them to read your will.

2. Both witnesses sign the will with you watching.

3. You date the will with the date of signing.

4. Both you and the witnesses should initial the bottom right hand corner of each page, except the page on which you sign.

Some don'ts

- Don't cheat! It could make the will invalid; and remember, a beneficiary who witnesses cannot inherit under your will.
- Don't staple or clip any other document to your will (but it's fine to put related documents in the same envelope).
- Don't cross anything out or make any alterations either before or after signing. They could make your will invalid.
- Don't try to add a PS after signing. It could make your will invalid.
- And don't try to make your will in anything other than in writing (video and audio wills are not yet acceptable!).

If you've slipped up – tear the whole thing up, download a fresh form from our website and start again.

Hang on! What happens if ...

You cannot read your will, or write your signature?

As long as you have the mental capacity to do so, you can make a will regardless of your ability – physical or mental – to read or write. If you cannot read the will, it should be read over to you and you should confirm that you understand it before it is signed. If you are unable to write, the will can be signed by someone else on your behalf (eg, Adam Smith on behalf of John Locke). The signature should be witnessed by two witnesses as before, and the signature clause should use a special form of wording which describes what has been done. We provide this form of words on page 135.

Have you got it all together?

Your will itself is only part of what you need to ensure that your assets go the people you want. Here is a checklist of loose ends that you may need to tie up:

- *Joint property* – remember, if you want to leave your share to someone in your will, you can only do so if 'the rule of survivorship' does not apply. See page 101 and if appropriate keep a copy of the notice to disapply the rule of survivorship with your will.
- *Death in service benefit* – if you die in harness, there may be a lump sum available from your pension fund. This payment is often discretionary, that is, it is up to the trustees of your pension fund to decide how much to pay, and to whom. However, they will take your expressed wishes into account – as long, of course, as they are aware of your wishes! Ask your employers for the contact details of the trustees and tell them who you would like to benefit.
- *Pensions* – if you are married, your widow/widower will often receive a proportion of your pension after your death. If you are unmarried, your partner will not automatically receive this, but you can often nominate them. Contact the pension fund trustees to make your wishes clear. Note that if you are estranged from your spouse but not fully divorced, you cannot nominate anyone else to receive your pension benefits.

- *Life insurance policies* – see page 42 on policies written in trust. The advantage of this type of policy is that the proceeds do not form part of your estate and are paid direct to the person you name in the trust deed that is attached to the policy. Have you done this?
- *Organ donation* – have you registered with the NHS Organ Donor scheme and do you carry a donor card? (see page 72).
- *Giving your body for medical teaching* – have you filled in an authorisation form? (see page 139).
- *List of assets* – (see page 30) if no one knows about them, your beneficiaries may never inherit. Put the list with your will.
- *Contact details* (see page 81) – anyone who needs to be aware of your death.
- Finally, DESTROY any previous will!

Keeping your will under review

A will 'speaks from death' (see page 24). The will you make today may be out of date in no time at all. For example:

- You marry, which will cancel any existing will (unless you expressly state that it is written with your marriage in mind – see page 135).
- You divorce, which will cancel any benefit for your former spouse – see page 62.
- You are in the throes of divorce proceedings, which will *not* cancel any benefit to your estranged spouse if you die before the decree absolute – see page 60.
- A beneficiary dies before you – what will happen to their legacy?
- Births, marriages and deaths – you want to benefit different people.
- The assets you now own are much more, much less, or different than when you last made a will. Inheritance Tax may suddenly become important to you. Or you may not be able to be as generous as before. And remember that a gift of a specific asset will lapse if you do not own it when you die. It may seem a little heartless to leave someone an item you no longer own, but maybe that's what you want.

- Changes in Inheritance Tax – if your will has been written with tax saving in mind, changes in tax law may blow your plans.
- Accidental destruction – whoops! If you destroy your will on purpose, that will cancel it. If it is an accident – eg the dog chews up the signed original of your will, there will, even if there is a copy in existence, be practical difficulties. Write and sign a new one.

Safe keeping

In the 1950s our local amateur dramatic society staged a play called *Where There's a Will*, which chronicled the adventures of a family unable to locate their dad's will. The will eventually turned up in the teapot – after they had all settled down for a reviving cuppa.

You need to keep your will somewhere sensible and easily accessible. You could ask your bank to take care of your will, but they will charge you. And if you choose to deposit your will with your bank, make sure your family know it is there.

For a fee of £15 (as of April 2001) you can take your will to your local Probate Registry or post it to the Principal Registry (see *Useful Contacts*). It can keep your will safe and produce it for your executors on request. This is perhaps the safest bet of all.

BUT remember to tell your family where your will is – probate registrars don't scan the obituaries columns and contact the bereaved families on their own initiative!

A word on various beneficiaries

Charities

Gifts to charities are free of Inheritance Tax – and below we show you how to make the taxman add to the gift.

If you plan to leave something to a charity, do make sure you get the name of the charity right. Many charities have names that are confusingly similar. For example, it would be easy to confuse Child*line* with Child*link*. Both exist. Some charities even change their names altogether. What was once the Spastics Society is now SCOPE.

Fortunately, leaving money to a charity, even one which changes its name twice yearly, is not as difficult as it sounds, because all registered charities, like cars, have numbers. Your gift will reach its intended destination if you put in the charity number to avoid confusion. For example, MENCAP (the Royal Society for Mentally Handicapped Children and Adults) is registered charity no. 222377.

There are over 186,000 registered charities, and not all

charities are registered (the main 'outsiders' are small charities whose annual income does not exceed £1,000). The Charity Commissioners maintains a full list of registered charities and you can consult it on line (see *Useful Contacts*). *The Charities Digest* lists only the main national and regional charities (see *Useful Contacts*). Local authorities should maintain lists of local charities. The wording of a gift to charity should cover the situation where the charity changes its name or amalgamates with another one, or even ceases to exist. Our charity clause provides for this (see page 118).

Many charities have a preferred form of wording for legacies to them. Call your chosen charity's legacy officer for advice.

—A present from the taxman

The trick is to make use of the income tax relief known as 'gift aid'. Instead of making the gift to charity in your will, do it during your lifetime. The effect of the gift aid legislation is to add the basic rate of tax to the amount that the charity gets – and you can set the gift against any high rate tax for which you may otherwise be liable.

If you want to make the gift in your will, you can still take advantage of the gift aid scheme by leaving the money to a *trusted* relation or friend (that is, one who will not pocket the money!) with a request for them to pass the money on to your chosen charity. The gift will still qualify for the Inheritance Tax exemption on your death, and the taxman treats the onward gift by your representative as net of income tax. The charity reclaims at the basic rate of tax, and your representative can claim the higher rate. We show you how to do this.

Beneficiaries with learning disabilities or mental health problems

If you want to do your best for someone with a learning disability or a mental health problem, it may well be inappropriate to leave them money outright. A person who lacks the mental capacity to handle money cannot give a receipt to your executors and, unless other arrangements are made, the money must be paid to someone appointed by the Public Guardianship Office as receiver.

Also, many state benefits are means tested and are not available to people with what the state regards as too much money. The current capital limit for people on Income Support is (as of 9 April 2001) £6,000. In other words, your beneficiary can have £6,000 in capital without losing out on their benefits.

If they have capital of between £6,000.01 and £12,000 (inclusive), every £250 above £6,000 is assumed to be earning a weekly income of £1, which is then deducted from their benefits. The limits are different for people in residential care. More details are available on >http://www.dss.gov.uk<. So a gift to a beneficiary who is receiving state benefits may push them over the limit, and not help them at all.

The usual way of providing for someone who is unable to manage money unaided, or who may be careless with money, is to make what is called a discretionary trust. This is an arrangement by which the beneficiary has no right to the money, but the trustees can use the money, or the income from the money, for his or her benefit. In practice, this enables the trustees to provide the beneficiary with extras and treats. Only actual payments affect the beneficiary's entitlement to benefit.

The trust will last for the lifetime of the beneficiary and you should specify who should get any money that is left over when the beneficiary dies.

For significant amounts of money, there are Capital Gains Tax advantages for trusts which comply with strict rules. For lesser amounts, the trustees' annual Capital Gains Tax exemption may be sufficient to avoid CGT.

You need to think carefully about who the trustees should be. Remember that professional trustees will want to charge for their services. If the beneficiary is looked after by a charity, there are other solutions available. These include:

- Leaving the money to the trustees of that charity, although you will want to be satisfied that the arrangement will in fact help your beneficiary.
- Using the services of the Trust Department of the Charities Aid Foundation (details in *Useful*

Contacts), which acts as an intermediary, with significant tax advantages.

- In the case of a mentally handicapped beneficiary, appointing the National Trustees for the Mentally Handicapped Ltd (a company operated by MENCAP). But note that the company will not act as an executor or with family members as trustees, and only administers trusts set up in its standard form (see MENCAP in *Useful Contacts*). In the case of a beneficiary with schizophrenia, using the similar scheme offered by the National Schizophrenia Fellowship (NSF) – see *Useful Contacts* for details.
- Setting up a charitable trust account administered by the Charities Aid Foundation. This confers the tax advantages which charities enjoy, and ensures continuity of trustees. The money cannot be spent directly on the beneficiary, but CAF undertakes to ensure that the money is passed to whichever charity is involved in the beneficiary's care, to use for their welfare. For further details contact CAF (see *Useful Contacts*).

MIND, the mental health charity, also offers the free booklet *Making Provision: planning your loved one's financial future.* The booklet won a 'Plain English' award and its author, a district judge with a mentally disabled son, explains clearly the kinds of trust that are available.

None of this is DIY stuff, however, and you will need professional advice.

If you think you want to make a gift to CAF, do it during your lifetime, because you can then do so under the gift aid legislation which adds the basic rate of tax to the amount that the charity gets. See *A present from the taxman* on page 94.

Wills by mentally incapable people

Generally, it takes mental capacity ('testamentary capacity') to make a valid will – which means that the testator must understand what they are doing, roughly how much they own and who ought to benefit from their will.

People who do not have mental capacity to make a will are not, however, helpless; because the Court of Protection can do it for them. If you have read up to this point, you have the necessary mental capacity to make your will; but you may know someone who could benefit from this procedure. Seek professional advice.

Bankrupt or irresponsible beneficiaries

If you leave money to someone who is bankrupt or under threat of bankruptcy, your legacy will go towards paying off their debts and your intended beneficiary will get nothing (unless, of course, the legacy is enough to pay off all their debts and still leave something over).

The classic solution is what is called a 'protective trust'. This gives the beneficiary the right to income for life, but in the event of bankruptcy the right to income is replaced by a discretionary trust (see *Buzzwords*). Care is needed in the drafting of a protective trust, and realistically, if you face this problem you should take professional advice.

There may be other, simpler solutions, for example leaving money to the bankrupt's spouse, partner or children.

For beneficiaries who are irresponsible with money, but are unlikely to become bankrupt, the right to income but not capital (that is, a life interest in the money) may be the solution. Again, you should seek professional advice.

Joint property – tying up the loose ends

Earlier on, we mentioned the rule of survivorship, and if you've forgotten what we said about it and also on joint tenants and tenants in common, see page 42.

If you do not want the rule of survivorship to apply, you must sign a document saying so. An example of this form is below.

You can also, of course, download as many copies as you wish from our website. You need to complete it; then you *must* give copies to the other co-owner(s) of the property. It is also helpful to put a copy of the document in the envelope with your will.

Where the asset is real estate, you can also notify the Land Registry and it will make an entry on the register for the property. You can find details of your local Land Registry by accessing the website on >www.landreg.gov.uk<.

Joint Property – Notice to Disapply Rule of Survivorship

From: [your name and address]

____

To: [co-owner's name and address]

____

Property: [identify co-owned property]:

I give you notice that from today the rule of survivorship is not to apply to the above property, and that it is now owned between us as beneficial tenants in common in the following shares:

My share [ ] %

Your share [ ]%

Signed ....

Dated ....

I acknowledge receipt of the original notice, of which this is a copy.

Signed..............................

Dated ....

Which will is right for you?

These simple questions should help you to choose the right will for your needs.

Do you have a partner?

If the answer is yes, consider Wills 1, 3 and 4.

Do you want to leave everything to your partner?

If the answer is yes, Will 1 is for you IF – but only if – you do not have children to consider.

Do you have children?

If the answer is yes, consider Wills 2 and 3.

Do you want to leave everything to your partner, *but* if your partner dies first, everything to your children?

If the answer is yes, you need Will 3.

Do you want to leave everything to your partner, *but* if your partner dies first, everything to a person or persons other than your children, or to charity?

If the answer is yes, consider Will 4.

Do you want to leave everything to charity?

If the answer is yes, you need Will 5.

Do you want to do something that is not covered in this book?

—You need professional advice.

WILLS

All of these wills can be found on our website and you can download as many as you want.

Do have a 'dry run' before you invite in your witnesses!

Administrative provisions

Apart from saying who is to get what, a well written will should tell your executors how to administer your estate. Most wills drown in oceans of verbiage to do this. We have cut all that out, but when necessary we have referred to the excellent Standard Provisions of the Society of Trust and Estate Practitioners. The incorporated provisions are the engine in the car and they are there for a reason. They work, but they do not need to be on display.

Will 1

This is the will to use if you want to leave everything to your husband, wife or partner (including your same-sex partner) and appoint them your sole executor.

Wills in which spouses or partners leave their entire estates to each other are often called mirror wills. This will is reproduced on the website and you can print off as many copies as you wish.

Points to consider

- What is to happen if your spouse or partner dies before you? If you want to make a substitutional gift, then add clause 2 from *Twiddly bits* on page 133.
- Otherwise there will be an intestacy (see *Buzzwords* and the Intestacy diagram on page 9 on the second death.
- What is to happen if your spouse or partner dies very shortly after you? The effect will be to 'bunch' your assets into your spouse or partner's estate. This may not cause any problems unless:
  - You and your spouse or partner would want to benefit different people after you are both dead;
  - The joint estate is worth more than the nil rate band for Inheritance Tax (see page 33). If it is, you may find that Inheritance Tax becomes payable on the second death: tax that is avoidable with careful planning.

The solution to these problems is to make the gift to your spouse or partner conditional on their surviving for, say, 30 days after you die (see *Twiddly bits* on page 136).

- Consider also whether or not you should appoint a substitute executor in case your spouse or partner dies before you, or is unable to take on the job.
- Do you and your spouse/partner intend to write mutual (mirror) wills? (see page 140).

Will of [insert your full name]

I [insert your full name] ______________________________

of [insert your full address] ______________________________

____

revoke all earlier wills and declare this to be my last will ('my Will').

I give the whole of my estate to [insert your spouse or partner's full name] and appoint [insert your spouse or partner's full name] as my sole executor.

Funeral arrangements

____

Dating, signing and witnessing

Date...

My Signature ....

I have signed my Will to give it effect in the presence of the two witnesses named below; and both of them have signed it in my presence.

Witness 1
Signature: ______________________________

Full name: ______________________________

Address: ______________________________

Occupation: ______________________________

Witness 2
Signature: ______________________________

Full name: ______________________________

Address: ______________________________

Occupation: ______________________________

Will 2

This is the will to use if you wish to leave everything to your children.

The will is reproduced on the website and you can print off as many copies as you wish.

Points to consider

- Is it possible that you might have more children before you die? Remember that both men and women can now have children at advanced ages. Leave your options open in your will by referring to 'my children' rather than naming them individually.
- If you have children under 18, you may want to appoint guardians (see page 51).
- If you have a child with special needs (see page 95).
- What is to happen if all your children die before you and they do not themselves leave any children? Consider a back-up option – a 'default beneficiary'.

Legal lore

- In the case of an outright gift to a child under 18, your will must provide for someone else to give the executors a receipt for the money, because the child cannot do so.
- In the form we use, all your children – legitimate, illegitimate or adopted – are equal under your will BUT a child whom you treat as your own, but of whom you are not the parent, such as a stepchild, will not benefit

automatically. You should make special provision for such children, mentioning them by name.

Will of [insert your full name] ______

I [insert your full name] ______

of [insert your full address] ______

______

revoke all earlier wills and declare this to be my last will ('my Will').

1. Executors and trustees

1.1. I appoint as my executors [insert full name] ______

of [insert address] ______

and [insert full name] ______

of [insert address]. ______

1.2. In my Will the expression 'my trustees' means the executors of my Will and the trustees of any trusts arising under it.

2. Guardians (only if you have children under 18) ______

I appoint [insert full name] ______

of [insert address ______

and [insert full name ______

of [insert address] ______

as guardians of any of my children who are under 18 when I die.

3. Trustees' duties and powers

My trustees are to hold my estate on trust to retain or sell it and:

3.1. to pay my debts, the cost of my funeral and the expenses of administering my estate;

3.2. to pay any taxes arising from my death;

3.3. to distribute the gifts and give effect to the other beneficial intentions of my Will.

My trustees are to have all the powers that the law and my Will confer for these purposes, and they are to exercise those powers with reasonable skill and care. If they need help, they are to seek professional advice and assistance.

4. Residuary gift

Subject as above, my trustees are to divide my estate equally among those of my children who survive me and attain the age of 18.
But if any of my children dies before me, or before age 18, leaving children, then those children shall on attaining the age of 18 take equally the share which their parent would otherwise have taken.

Incorporated provisions

The *Standard Provisions of the Society of Trust and Estate Practitioners* (1st edition) are to apply.

Funeral arrangements

Dating, signing and witnessing

Date...

My Signature ....

I have signed my Will to give it effect in the presence of the two witnesses named below; and both of them have signed it in my presence.

Witness 1
Signature: ______________________________

Full name: ______________________________

Address: ______________________________

Occupation: ______________________________

Witness 2
Signature: ______________________________

Full name: ______________________________

Address: ______________________________

Occupation: ______________________________

Will 3

This is the will to use if you want to leave everything to your partner, and if your partner dies first, everything to your children.

In respect of the gift to your partner, see the comments on Will 1.

In respect of the gift to your children, see the comments on Will 2.

—If you and your spouse or partner are not both the mother and the father of all the children (for example if there are stepchildren), the form of will below may not benefit all the children you have in mind. Seek professional advice.

The will is reproduced on the website and you can print off as many copies as you wish.

Will of [insert your full name] ____________________

I [insert your full name] ____________________

of [insert your full address] ____________________

____

revoke all earlier wills and declare this to be my last will ('my Will').

Part 1

I give the whole of my estate to [insert your spouse or partner's full name] ____________________

and appoint [insert your full address] ____________________

____

[insert your spouse's or partner's full name] as my sole executor ____________________

____

BUT if this gift fails then the provisions of Part 2 of my Will shall apply instead of Part 1.

Part 2

1. Executors and trustees

1.1. I appoint as my executors [insert full name] ____________________

of [insert address] ____________________

and [insert full name] ____________________

of [insert address]. ____________________

1.2. In my Will the expression 'my trustees' means the executors of my Will and the trustees of any trusts arising under it.

2. Guardians (only if you have children under 18)

I appoint [insert full name] ____________________

of [insert address] ____________________

and [insert full name] ____________________

of [insert address] ____

as guardians of any of my children who are under 18 when I die.

3. Trustees' duties and powers

My trustees are to hold my estate on trust to retain or sell it and:

3.1. to pay my debts, the cost of my funeral and the expenses of administering my estate;

3.2. to pay any taxes arising from my death;

3.3. to distribute the gifts and give effect to the other beneficial intentions of my Will.

My trustees are to have all the powers that the law and my Will confer for these purposes, and they are to exercise those powers with reasonable skill and care. If they need help, they are to seek professional advice and assistance.

4. Residuary gift

Subject as above, my trustees are to divide my estate equally among those of my children who survive me and attain the age of 18.

But if any of my children dies before me, or before age 18, leaving children, then those children shall on attaining the age of 18 take equally the share which their parent would otherwise have taken.

Part 3

The provisions of Part 3 of my Will are of general application, and apply whether Part 1 or Part 2 applies.

Incorporated provisions

The *Standard Provisions of the Society of Trust and Estate Practitioners* (1st edition) are to apply.

Funeral arrangements

Dating, signing and witnessing

Date……………………………………………

My Signature ……………………………………

I have signed my Will to give it effect in the presence of the two witnesses named below; and both of them have signed it in my presence.

Witness 1

Signature: ______________________________

Full name: ______________________________

Address: ______________________________

Occupation: ______________________________

Witness 2

Signature: ______________________________

Full name: ______________________________

Address: ______________________________

Occupation: ______________________________

Will 4

This is the will to use if you want to leave everything to your partner, but if your partner dies first, everything to other beneficiaries or charity.

In respect of a gift to your spouse or partner, see the notes for Will 1.

In respect of gifts to charity, see pages 93–95 on this subject

Gifts to charity are exempt from Inheritance Tax. Gifts to people, other than your spouse, are not exempt, although no tax may be payable as long as your estate does not exceed the nil rate band (see page 33). There are potential tax problems if you divide your residuary estate between exempt and non-exempt beneficiaries. If you think this may apply to you, take professional advice.

The will is reproduced on the website and you can print off as many copies as you wish.

Will of [insert your full name] ______________________

I [insert your full name] ______________________

of [insert your full address] ______________________

____

revoke all earlier wills and declare this to be my last will ('my Will').

Part 1

I give the whole of my estate to [insert your spouse or partner's full name] ______________________

and appoint ______________________

____

[insert your spouse's or partner's full name] as my sole executor

____

BUT if this gift fails then the provisions of Part 2 of my Will shall apply instead of Part 1.

Part 2

1. Executors and trustees

1.1. I appoint as my executors [insert full name] ______________________

of [insert address] ______________________

and [insert full name] ______________________

of [insert address]. ______________________

1.2. In my Will the expression 'my trustees' means the executors of my Will and the trustees of any trusts arising under it.

2. Trustees' duties and powers

My trustees are to hold my estate on trust to retain or sell it and:

2.1. to pay my debts, the cost of my funeral and the expenses of administering my estate;

2.2. to pay any taxes arising from my death;

2.3. to distribute the gifts and give effect to the other beneficial intentions of my Will.

My trustees are to have all the powers that the law and my Will confer for these purposes, and they are to exercise those powers with reasonable skill and care. If they need help, they are to seek professional advice and assistance.

3. Residuary gift

Subject as above, my trustees are to divide and pay the residue of my estate as follows:

3.1. [ ]% to [insert name and address of charity, and charity number]

3.2. [ ]% to [insert name and address of charity, and charity number]

3.3. [ ]% to [insert name and address of charity, and charity number]

3.4. [ ]% to [insert name and address of charity, and charity number]

Even if any charity named in my Will changes its name or constitution, or amalgamates with another charity, it is still to receive the benefit given by my Will.

If any charity named in my Will has ceased to exist, the benefit is to be given to another charity, selected by my trustees, and having the same or similar charitable purposes.

Part 3

The provisions of Part 3 of my Will are of general application, and apply whether Part 1 or Part 2 applies.

Incorporated provisions

The *Standard Provisions of the Society of Trust and Estate Practitioners* (1st edition) are to apply.

Funeral arrangements

Dating, signing and witnessing

Date……………………………………………

My Signature ………………………………….

I have signed my Will to give it effect in the presence of the two witnesses named below; and both of them have signed it in my presence.

Witness 1
Signature: ______________________________

Full name: ______________________________

Address: ______________________________

Occupation: ______________________________

Witness 2
Signature: ______________________________

Full name: ______________________________

Address: ______________________________

Occupation: ______________________________

Will 5

This is the will to use if you want to leave everything to charity.

In respect of gifts to charity, see pages 93–95 on this subject.

The will is reproduced on the website and you can print off as many copies as you wish.

Will of [insert your full name] ______________________________

I [insert your full name] ______________________________

of [insert your full address] ______________________________

____

revoke all earlier wills and declare this to be my last will ('my Will').

1. Executors and trustees

1.1. I appoint as my executors [insert full name] ______________________________

of [insert address] ______________________________

and [insert full name] ______________________________

of [insert address]. ______________________________

2. Trustees' duties and powers

My trustees are to hold my estate on trust to retain or sell it and:

2.1. to pay my debts, the cost of my funeral and the expenses of administering my estate;

2.2. to pay any taxes arising from my death;

2.3. to distribute the gifts and give effect to the other beneficial intentions of my Will.

My trustees are to have all the powers that the law and my Will confer for these purposes, and they are to exercise those powers with reasonable skill and care. If they need help, they are to seek professional advice and assistance.

3. Residuary gift

Subject as above, my trustees are to divide and pay the residue of my estate as follows:

3.1. [ ]% to [insert name and address of charity, and charity number] ______________________________

3.2. [ ]% to [insert name and address of charity, and charity number] ______________________________

3.3. [ ]% to [insert name and address of charity, and charity number] ______________________________

3.4. [ ]% to [insert name and address of charity, and charity number] ______

Even if any charity named in my Will changes its name or constitution, or amalgamates with another charity, it is still to receive the benefit given by my Will.

If any charity named in my Will has ceased to exist, the benefit is to be given to another charity, selected by my trustees, and having the same or similar charitable purposes.

Incorporated provisions

The *Standard Provisions of the Society of Trust and Estate Practitioners* (1st edition) are to apply.

Funeral arrangements

Dating, signing and witnessing

Date...

My Signature ....

I have signed my Will to give it effect in the presence of the two witnesses named below; and both of them have signed it in my presence.

Witness 1

Signature: ______

Full name: ______

Address: ______

Occupation: ______

Witness 2

Signature: ________________________________

Full name: ________________________________

Address: ________________________________

Occupation: ________________________________

Will 6

This is the type of will to use if you wish to leave everything to named beneficiaries other than charities

The main issue with this type of will is: what happens if a named beneficiary dies before you? In our form of will, we provide that the deceased beneficiary's share is divided pro rata between the surviving beneficiaries. An alternative would be for the deceased beneficiary's share to go to their spouse, partner or children.

Will of [insert your full name]

I [insert your full name]

of [insert your full address]

revoke all earlier wills and declare this to be my last will ('my Will').

1. Executors and trustees

1.1. I appoint as my executors [insert full name]

of [insert address]

and [insert full name]

of [insert address].

2. Trustees' duties and powers

My trustees are to hold my estate on trust to retain or sell it and:

2.1. to pay my debts, the cost of my funeral and the expenses of administering my estate;

2.2. to pay any taxes arising from my death;

2.3. to distribute the gifts and give effect to the other beneficial intentions of my Will.

My trustees are to have all the powers that the law and my Will confer for these purposes, and they are to exercise those powers with reasonable skill and care. If they need help, they are to seek professional advice and assistance.

3. Residuary gift

Subject as above, my trustees are to divide and pay the residue of my estate as follows:

3.1. [ ]% to [insert name and address of beneficiary]

3.2. [ ]% to [insert name and address of beneficiary]

3.3. [ ]% to insert name and address of beneficiary]

3.4. [ ]% to [insert name and address of beneficiary]

If any beneficiary named in my will dies before me, the deceased beneficiary's share is to be added pro rata to the shares of the other beneficiaries.

Incorporated provisions

The *Standard Provisions of the Society of Trust and Estate Practitioners* (1st edition) are to apply.

Funeral arrangements

Dating, signing and witnessing

Date...

My Signature ....

I have signed my Will to give it effect in the presence of the two witnesses named below; and both of them have signed it in my presence.

Witness 1
Signature: ____________________

Full name: ____________________

Address: ____________________

Occupation: ____________________

Witness 2
Signature: ____________________

Full name: ____________________

Address: ____________________

Occupation: ____________________

Will 7

This will provides a discretionary trust for a child with a mental disability. The distinguishing feature of a discretionary trust is that there is no one who can claim a right to the money, and the purpose of this is to protect the child's right to State benefits. Because the trust is discretionary, there have to be other potential beneficiaries – otherwise it creates what is known as a life interest in the money. One consequence of this is that unscrupulous trustees could divert the money away from the child with the disability. You must therefore be able to trust your trustees!

Before the trustees spend money for the disabled child's benefit, they should always see what other sources of funding (eg grants) may be available.

A discretionary trust for a disabled person offers important Inheritance Tax and Capital Gains Tax advantages – as long as

- at least half of the capital which is actually spent is spent for the benefit of the disabled person

- the income from the trust must not be available for the benefit of anyone except the disabled person (alternatively, the disabled person must be entitled actually to receive at least half the income).

These tax advantages are also available for a beneficiary who has a physical disability and receives associated benefits, typically Disability Living

Allowance.

Will of [insert your full name] ______

I [insert your full name] ______

of [insert your full address] ______

______

revoke all earlier wills and declare this to be my last will ('my Will').

1. Executors and trustees

1.1. I appoint as my executors [insert full name] ______

of [insert address] ______

and [insert full name] ______

of [insert address]. ______

2. Guardians (only if you have children under 18) ______

I appoint [insert full name] ______

of [insert address] ______

and [insert full name] ______

of [insert address] ______

as guardians of any of my children who are under 18 when I die.

3. Trustees' duties and powers

My trustees are to hold my estate on trust to retain or sell it and:

3.1. to pay my debts, the cost of my funeral and the expenses of administering my estate;

3.2. to pay any taxes arising from my death;

3.3. to distribute the gifts and give effect to the other beneficial intentions of my Will.

My trustees are to have all the powers that the law and my Will confer for these purposes, and they are to exercise those powers with reasonable skill and care. If they need help, they are to seek professional advice and assistance.

4. Discretionary legacy for children, including a child with a disability

4.1. In this legacy and the gift of residue:

'My child with special needs' means [insert name of disabled child]

'The trust gift' means: £

'The trust fund' means: the assets that my trustees hold on the terms of trust set out in this clause. The trust gift is the initial capital of the trust fund.

'The trust beneficiaries' means

- my child with special needs
- my other children
- the spouse of any of my children
- my grandchildren

4.2. If my child with special needs survives me, I give the trust gift free of taxes to my trustees on the terms set out in this legacy.

4.3. During the lifetime of my child with special needs my trustees are at their discretion to:

4.3.1 use all or part of the income from the trust fund for the benefit of my child with special needs, and for not more than 21 years to save any remaining income;

4.3.2. use the capital of the trust fund for the benefit of the trust beneficiaries, so long as not less than half is used for the benefit of my child with special needs.

4.4. As well as their implied powers, my trustees have the discretionary power to use all or any part of the capital and/or income of the trust fund for the benefit of my child with special needs to pay the cost of:

4.4.1. altering or adapting any living accommodation, whoever owns it, for the convenience and comfort of my child with special needs;

4.4.2. providing domestic appliances and/or domestic help for my child with special needs and/or for whoever is living with or caring for them at that time;

4.4.3. providing vehicles appropriate to the needs of my child with special needs and/or for whoever is living with or caring for them at that time;

4.4.4. providing holidays for my child with special needs and/or anyone living with or caring for them at that time.

4.5. My trustees can also use all or part of the income or capital of the trust fund to buy a financial product (such as an annuity) to provide financial security for my child with special needs, even though this may use the whole of the trust fund.

4.6. My trustees can allow any dwelling forming part of the trust fund to be used as a home for my child with special needs, either alone or with someone else. In the latter case, my trustees need not make the other person pay rent, so long as the arrangement benefits my child with special needs.

4.7. Upon the death of my child with special needs, my trustees can use money from the trust fund to pay the funeral expenses and also, at their discretion, the cost of a memorial.

4.8. After the death of my child with special needs, my trustees are to use the income and capital of the trust fund for the benefit of the other trust beneficiaries and within one year my trustees are at their discretion to distribute what remains of the trust fund to the other trust beneficiaries. In making this final distribution, my trustees need not ensure equality between my other beneficiaries, or benefit all of them.

5. Residuary gift to children other than my child with special needs

Subject as above, my trustees are to divide my estate equally among those of my children, other than my child with special needs, who survive me and attain the age of 18. If any of my children dies before me, or before age 18, leaving children, then those children shall on attaining the age of 18 take equally the share which their parent would otherwise have taken.

Incorporated provisions

The *Standard Provisions of the Society of Trust and Estate Practitioners* (1st edition) are to apply.

Funeral arrangements

Dating, signing and witnessing

Date……………………………………………

My Signature ………………………………….

I have signed my Will to give it effect in the presence of the two witnesses named below; and both of them have signed it in my presence.

Witness 1
Signature: ______________________________

Full name: ______________________________

Address: ______________________________

Occupation: ______________________________

Witness 2
Signature: ______________________________

Full name: ______________________________

Address: ______________________________

Occupation: ______________________________

____

Twiddly bits

These extra clauses are to our basic wills what the sprig of parsley or cherry tomato is to a restaurant meal.

1. Specific legacies

Examples of specific legacies might be £1,000, a piece of jewellery or a car. There are traps with this type of legacy:

(a) In the case of a gift other than money, is the description in your will sufficient to identify the asset?

(b) Will you still own the same asset when you die? If you do not, the gift will lapse (see page 24) unless you describe your gift by reference to the category of asset that you own when you die. An example is 'the car which I own at the time of my death'. Our term for this is a gift of a mutable asset (if it seems pompous to you, try thinking of something better).

Even then, the gift may still lapse if by the time you die you do not own anything in that category.

(c) If you own – or may own at the time of your death – more than one diamond necklace/car/boat, how will your executors know which one you have in mind?

(d) Are you sure the item is yours to leave (i.e. not on HP etc)?

(e) If you are rich enough to have to pay Inheritance Tax (see page 32), will the person who gets the asset have to pay Inheritance Tax on it?

Here are some sample clauses.

Gift of fixed amount of money

I give to [name] of [address] [£] [free of Inheritance Tax].

Gift of specific asset

I give to [name] of [address] [free of Inheritance Tax] my [describe item fully].

Gift of mutable asset

I give to [name] of [address] the [ ] which I own at the time of my death [free of Inheritance Tax]

Legal lore

'Mutable' comes from the Latin *mutare* to change. The reason for adding 'which I own at the time of my death' is that the Morris Minor you own now may have mutated into an Aston Martin by the time you die.

2. Substitutional gift

Suppose you leave a gift to someone, but they die before you? In the case of a specific gift, the money or goods will go back into the general pot – unless you provide for the gift to pass to someone else in substitution. This is a substitutional gift. Here is the wording:

I give free of taxes [say what you are giving] to [name and address] but if he/she dies before me I give it to [name and address].

For examples of substitutional gifts of residue, see 3 and 4 overleaf.

2. Children – receipt for gift

You can leave gifts to children under 18, but they cannot give your executors a valid receipt. This means that the executors cannot safely hand over the gift unless the will provides for someone else to give the receipt. Here is a clause with a gift to grandchildren, with provision for a receipt.

I give (£100) free of Inheritance Tax to each of my grandchildren living at the date of my death. In the case of a grandchild under 18 the grandchild's parent or guardian can give a valid receipt to my executors.

3. Children – a clean slate

You may have made gifts to your children during your lifetime. Do you want these gifts to affect what they get under your will?

Legal lore

This is known as *hotchpot* (which later became *hotch-potch* or – in the USA – *hodge-podge*). Hotchpot comes from old French *hocher* to shake – and *pot* – a pot. Not a lot of people know that...

If you do, adjust your children's shares accordingly when you make your will, ie leave less to the child who has already had a cut.

If you don't wish to do this, add a clause as follows:

In ascertaining the entitlement of each of my children under my Will, no account is to be taken of previous gifts made by me or by their other parent.

4. Will made in anticipation of marriage

I am expecting to marry [insert name].

My Will is to have immediate effect, and is not to be revoked by my marriage to [insert name].

5. Signature clause for blind testator

Date ……………………………………

Signature of [insert person's name] signing on my behalf

……………………………………………

As I am blind, my Will has been read aloud to me. I understand and approve it. I have authorised [insert person's name] to give my Will effect by signing it in my presence and in the presence of the two witnesses named below; and both of them have signed it in our presence.

Witness 1
Signature: ______________________

Full name: ______________________

Address: ______________________

Occupation: ______________________

Witness 2
Signature: ______________________

Full name: ______________________

Address: ______________________

Occupation: ______________________

6. The 30-day clause

On condition that [insert your spouse or partner's full name] survives me by 30 days, I give the whole of my estate to [insert your spouse or partner's full name] and appoint [insert your spouse or partner's full name] as my sole executor.

Of course, if you use the 30-day clause, you really must set out what will happen to your estate if you outlive your partner, or they die within 30 days of your death.

7. Funeral arrangements

Remember, your wishes are not binding on your executors. All the same, many people derive great comfort from planning their funerals, including the music to be played and a lavish wake for the mourners.

Legal lore

A wake was originally an all-night watch over a corpse, during which the mourners would take turns to pray over the body by candlelight and protect it from harm (body snatchers!). After the funeral, this vigil was followed by feasting. At modern wakes the vigil is optional but the feasting is still popular.

Here are some typical clauses:

I should like my body to be cremated.

I should like my body to be buried at [name]. *Be specific and check that space is available. In some churchyards and cemeteries you can pay in advance to reserve a plot.*

I should like my body to be buried next to my late husband/wife [name]. *Be specific here, especially if you have been married more than once!*

No flowers, please; instead, donations may be made to [name and number of charity].

I would like a green burial with a tree on my grave as a memorial. If my executors do not know how to arrange this, or the location of the nearest suitable site, they can find out from an organisation such as the Natural Death Centre, telephone number 0208 8208 2853.

You may like to refer to *Funeral Arrangements* on page 65–70 for inspiration.

Or indeed you could delegate the whole thing to your executors: 'I should like my executors to make such funeral arrangement as they think appropriate'.

8. Organ donation

Your will is not the place to raise this issue for the first time (see page 71). Here, however, is a clause to include in your will:

'I wish to donate all or any of my organs for transplant or other medical purposes, if required. If the hospital removes organs but does not make use of them, it may retain or destroy them at its discretion'.

9. Donating your body for medical teaching

This again is something that if possible you should arrange in your lifetime, as it is helpful to establish in advance that there is a local medical school which will want your body (see page 75). As your will may not be read until after your funeral, it is of course sensible to let your family know your wishes. The law provides for you to make your wishes known either in writing or orally in the presence of two witnesses.

Here is a clause to put in your will.

'I wish to donate my body for anatomical examination after my death. If, in the course of the examinations, organs or tissue are removed, the medical school may retain or destroy them at its discretion. On completion of the anatomical examination, I wish my body to be [buried/cremated]'.

Here is a form of authorisation for you to complete in your lifetime and give to your family.

ANATOMY ACT 1984

AUTHORISATION FOR USE OF MY BODY FOR

ANATOMICAL EXAMINATION

TO MY EXECUTORS AND FAMILY

Full Name ....

Address ....

I wish to donate my body for anatomical examination after my death. If, in the course of the examinations, organs or tissue are removed, the medical school may retain or destroy them at its discretion. On completion of the anatomical examination, I wish my body to be [buried/cremated].

Here are the details of the medical school that may be able to use my body. [insert details]

Signature..

Date:..

10. Mutual wills *(see Buzzwords)*

You may think that a mutual will is a neat way of making sure that your assets are not diverted by your spouse or partner ofter your death, for example, to a new gold-digging lover, at the expense of your children. But think carefully, because there are severe practical problems.

- Do you intend the mutual wills to apply to assets which your spouse or partner acquires after your death?
- What happens if your spouse or partner remarries? Remember, marriage revokes a will.
- How is the agreement to be policed? Assets get bought and sold and mixed up with other assets; try unscrambling an omelette and you'll get some idea of the problems.
- What about lifetime gifts by the survivor after you die?

Apart from all this, a mutual will seeks to impose a straightjacket on your spouse or partner after your death. Is this really a good thing?

Here is a clause declaring that you and your partner are making mutual ('mirror') wills.

Declaration that wills are mutual

'My will is a mutual will with [name of husband/wife/partner], which he/she has signed at the same time that I have signed mine. We have agreed that neither of us during our joint lives or afterwards is to revoke (except by marriage) their will or to make any gift or settlement of any property or any further will or codicil which has a material adverse effect on any interest given by or under their will except during our joint lives by the written agreement of us both and after the death of one of us by the written agreement of each beneficiary whose interest is so affected. If either of us remarries they are to execute a further will containing such disposals as are necessary to give effect to the gifts made in our common wills. The new will does not need to apply to any property acquired by the survivor as a consequence of the remarriage but the survivor should keep such property separate from and not mixed with their other property'.

And here is a declaration that two wills are not mutual:

Declaration

Although [insert name] is making a will in the same or similar forms as I am, we agree that our wills are not binding on each other. We are each free to revoke our respective wills before or after the death of the other.

Useful contacts

Safe Keeping of Wills

For £15 (as of April 2001) the Princpal Registry can keep your will safe and produce it for executors on request.

Principal Registry
First Avenue House
42-49 High Holborn
London WC1V 6NP
Tel 020 7947 6000

Severing Joint Tenancies, etc

HM Land Registry
Website: *www.landreg.gov.uk*

Information about Inheritance Tax, etc

Inland Revenue website *www.inlandrevenue.gov.uk*

Finance for Guardians

Guardian's Allowance Unit
Child Benefit Centre
(Washington) PO Box 1
Newcastle upon Tyne
NE88 1AA
Telephone: 0191 225 1535, 0191 225 1536
Textphone: 0191 225 1833
Email: *Child-Benefit@MS04.dss.gov.uk*

Advice on Funerals

A Consumer's Guide to Funerals – there is a webste
www.oft.gov.uk/html/funerals

British Humanist Association
47 Theobalds Road
London WC1X 8XP

(non religious funerals}

The Natural Death Centre
20 Heber Road
London NW2 6AA
Tel 020 8208 2853
Email rhino@dial.pipex.com;
Web: www.naturaldeath.org.uk

(green burials, DIY funerals and many other things. It also edits the *New Natural Death Handbook*, editored by Nicholas Albery and Stephanie Wienrich of the Natural Death Centre; published by Rider at £10.99. ISBN 0-7126-0576-2)

Lesbian and Gay Christian Movement
Tel 020 7739 1249

(Christian funerals for gay people, including details of sympathetic clergy near you)

Muslim funerals

Mr Ebrahim Ahmed Jaset
Secretary
Muslim Burial Council of Leicestershire
394 East Park Road
Leicester LE5 5HL
Tel/Fax: 0116 273 0141
Mobile 07803 240492
Website www.mbcol.org.uk

Email: admin@mbcol.org.uk

Organ Donation

NHS Organ Donor Registration Forms

Department of Health Organ Donor
Literature Line
Tel: 0845 606400

Body Donation – Anatomy

HM Inspector of Anatomy
Department of Health
Wellington House
133–155 Waterloo Road
London SE1 8UG
Tel: 020 7972 4342

London Anatomy Office
Tel: 020 8846 1216

DSS Alexander Fleming House
Elephant and Castle
London SE1 6BY

Tissue Donation – Drug Research

Department of Histology
Peterborough District Hospital
Thorpe Road
Peterborough PE3 6DA
Tel: 01733 874000
www.tissuebank.co.uk

Living wills

Living Wills and Enduring Power of Attorney
Mark Fairweather and Rosy Border
The Stationery Office, 2001
ISBN 0 11 702819 3. £7.99

Enduring Power of Attorney

Living Wills and Enduring Power of Attorney
Mark Fairweather and Rosy Border
The Stationery Office, 2001
ISBN 0 11 702819 3. £7.99

Court of Protection

Customer Services Unit (Mental Health)
Public Guardianship Office
Protection Division
Stewart House
24 Kingsway
London WC2B 6JX
Tel: 020 7664 7000

Charities

Charity Commissioners
0870 333 0123 for central register.
Website: *www.charity-commission.gov.uk*

They can search for charities by name or by type of charity

Charities Digest
Published annually by Waterlow Information Services Ltd ISBN 1 85783 803 3

Charities Aid Foundation
Trust Department
Kings Hill
West Malling
Kent ME19 4TA
Tel: 01732 520000
Website: *www.cafonline.org*

MENCAP
National Centre
123 Golden Lane
London EC1Y 0RT
Tel: 020 7454 0454

National Schizophrenia Fellowship
NSF Trustees Ltd
28 Castle Street
Kingston-upon-Thames
Surrey KT1 1SS
Tel: 020 8547 3937

Index

Printed in the United Kingdom by The Stationery Office Ltd, London
TJ5194 C30 9/01